GameChangers℠

IMPROVISATION FOR BUSINESS
IN THE NETWORKED WORLD

McKava Press
Los Angeles

As we move from the rigid, hierarchical business structures of the Industrial Age to the fluid, non-linear models of the Networked World, GameChangers have never been more important or essential. Whenever teamwork, creativity, flexibility and problem-solving skills are necessary for success, these players step up.

They develop relationships that are good for business. They pay careful attention to details and at the same time have expansive worldviews. They are quick-on-their-feet, unflappable and in tune with their teammates, stakeholders and the marketplace.

They are the top performers in any organization — the best managers, the most resourceful employees, the culture-shapers. They play the game and make things happen.

In short, GameChangers are masters of improvisation in business.

GameChangers℠

IMPROVISATION FOR BUSINESS
IN THE NETWORKED WORLD

BY
MIKE BONIFER

For VeeVee and Fern

McKava Press

**GameChangers, – Improvisation for Business
in the Networked World**
by
Mike Bonifer

GameChangers, LLC
2658 Griffith Park Blvd
Suite 806
Los Angeles CA 90039-2520

www.gamechangers.com

Copyright © 2007 by Mike Bonifer. First Edition.

Library of Congress Cataloging/Publication Data

Bonifer, Mike

GameChangers – Improvisation for Business in the Networked World by Mike Bonifer. Includes Glossary, Index and Endnotes

ISBN- 978-0-9799489-0-9

I. Business Education—United States. I. Bonifer, Mike. Improvisation for business. II. Title. III. Title: Improvisation for business.

Contents

FOREWORD

I MET MY WIFE, SUE, WHEN WE WERE GROWING UP back in Fort Wayne, Indiana. She came from a better side of town, and it was a little scandalous for her to be dating someone from the semi-circus known as the Wall family. I say 'semi-circus' because I literally grew up inside a roller-skating rink. My 11 brothers and sisters, my parents and I, and a dog named Scout all lived and worked inside the RollerDome in Fort Wayne. You stepped out through a door in our family room onto a 20,000-square foot roller-skating rink made of 560,000 three-quarter inch strips of maple wood. I know, because my father, brothers and I laid every single one of those strips ourselves.

Most of what I know about improvising in business, I learned in my 19 years under the RollerDome. During that time, I saw the roller-skating business nearly die off completely and my family do all kinds of improvising just so we could keep the doors open. When new music, new skate technology and a new generation of people made roller disco popular, we improvised along with that, too, and made a lot of money during those years. With what I knew about skating rink floors, I got into the business of building portable music stages, and then into the concert production and promotion business, which in turn led me into many, many business ventures related to music and new media.

I follow opportunities and point them out to other people. We share the vision. We get things done. That's improvisation, and it's no different from what we did back at the RollerDome. This past year, on July 7, 2007, a lot of simultaneous opportunities and a vision shared by a lot of people culminated in *Live Earth – Concerts for a Climate in Crisis*, the biggest event of its kind in the history of the world.

On the day of Live Earth, Sue and I stood on the stage at Wembley Stadium in London – a stage made of recycled wood and decorated with used automobile tires! – and looked out at that crowd of 90,000 people moving together to the music, and we looked at each other with tears in our eyes and just shook our heads and smiled and said, "Can you believe it!?"

How far we had come. How far we still have to go.

Mike Bonifer has written a book that explains, among many other things, how a young person with nothing more than a dream and an idea about what he stands for can become successful in business and in life. That's my story, but it can be anyone's. The opportunities are there if you pay attention and act on them. That, to me, is what *GameChangers*, and improvisation in business is all about – recognizing opportunities minute-to-minute and acting on them. Mike's book is a brilliant guide for getting there.

Kevin Wall
Creator and Producer
Live Earth

I. The Reality Is...

Spontaneity is the moment of personal freedom when we are faced with a reality and see it, explore it and act accordingly.

— *Viola Spolin*

You Are an Improviser

WE DON'T KNOW WHAT WILL HAPPEN NEXT. It is as true today as it ever was.

Who will be the next person to call you on the telephone? The next to email you? The next person you encounter face-to-face — who will it be and what will he or she say to you? When life takes the next left turn, with what unexpected tide of events will you collide? No way of knowing, is there? The future is unscripted.

The next time you pitch your product — how will the conversation go? If you're a good salesperson, you will admit that you do not know. You will react fluidly to your situation, responding to what the customer wants, their perceptions, emotions, attitudes and desires. None of this will be known to you before you encounter that customer. The two of you will reach an agreement and together paint a picture of a vision of the future you and the customer share. When you close the sale, it is not so much your product you will have sold, it is a future that includes your product in the customer's life — maybe even a future that would not be possible without your product.

When you hire your next employee, what will you see that convinces you the candidate is right for the job? What will he or she say? What will interest you about them? If you're a strong recruiter, you don't know. The people you hire surprise you. They perform in ways that cause them to stand out from the pack. And you don't really know ahead of time what the standout features of their performances will be. You might know it when you see it, but not before. It is not something you can quantify. The intangibles make great employees and that's what you're looking for – the fire that burns inside the people who give you confidence, who expand the possibilities a degree or two, who crack open doorways to new perceptions, new worlds. So you pay attention. And you conduct the interview without any expectations, waiting to be surprised. This kind of human communication cannot be scripted or preordained. It arises spontaneously from interactions between people.

When you invest time and money in a business objective, what convinces you to do so? If you are honest with yourself, you acknowledge that the best and most rewarding decisions come from your gut. If good business decisions came from the brain, really smart people would never make really dumb decisions. And we know that they do. Good businesspeople trust instincts informed by experience, knowledge and awareness of the world in which they conduct their business. They pay attention, then take decisive action. They realize there are infinite ways to achieve a goal and they're open to all of them. That's good business. That's improvisation.

Business can't get done without the ability to improvise. Successful businesspeople are, as a rule, excellent improvisers. And the most accomplished of them are not only business superstars, they also give themselves the best chance for happiness and success throughout their lives. They forge paths in which their *work* ethic and *personal* ethic coincide.

Points of Clarity

GameChangers gives you the keys to the performance-based discipline that will be the measure of the successful business organization in the Networked World. It is a practical guide to business communication. It will help you become more entrepreneurial, observant, creative and contributory in everything you do.

The first point of clarity for understanding improvisation in business is this: *You are already an improviser.*

Like the improvisers who perform on theatrical stages, business people participate every day in 'scenes' involving two or more people that are largely if not entirely unscripted. When you have a conversation with someone you're meeting for the first time, you're improvising. Every time you introduce a breakthrough idea to your organization or turn an idea into action, that's improv. When you're spontaneous, you're improvising. When you brainstorm, make a sales pitch that departs from the script, collaborate with your coworkers to resolve a business problem, do a PowerPoint presentation without reading what's on the slides, interview for a job (or conduct the interview), deal with a grievance, train a new employee or launch a brand, you are calling on many of the skills improv performers use to build their scenes.

But wait a second – isn't improv about getting laughs? Isn't that the reason it exists? Well, not exactly. The improv performed today on stage and TV has its origins in childhood education in 1920s Chicago. Only by a few simple twists of fate did it become a well-known engine for cranking out comedy. The applications of improvisation are far broader than what most people think of when they hear the word 'improv'. In these pages, you will see how the set of skills that have been used in improv comedy for over half a century can greatly enhance your business performance.

Which brings us to a second point of clarity: *Improvisation is a set of skills that can be studied, practiced and improved upon.*

These skills, taken together, comprise an approach to business communications, personal productivity and teamwork that is tailor-made for the Networked World. Learning the *GameChangers* fundamentals will help you get better at what you do, eliminate weaknesses in your game, and allow you to have a strong say in your professional destiny.

Suppose you want to learn a craft. Let's say it's sailing. Imagine if the way you set about learning to sail is by crewing. You do your job well and fit in smoothly with your fellow crew members. You grew up near the ocean, enjoy being on the water and welcome the drama that comes with treacherous weather. You stay fit. You love the lifestyle. You learn how to tie the hell out of many different kinds of knots. But…you don't anticipate the weather; that's someone else's job. You don't study oceanographic maps; they are not required for you to perform your duties. You don't pick the brains of other sailors for anything except bawdy stories of good times past. You don't understand the computers used by the captain to plot your course; they're down below and you're a topsider. You don't read books about sailing; you're more of a learn-by-doing person.

You don't keep up with developments in keel and sail construction; the owners look after that. So you never really learn how to sail. You learn how to crew.

Yet this is how many of us acquire the skills we use in business. We are 'on the boat', learning in a master/apprentice dynamic that dates back to the Middle Ages, and we trust that it's enough. We memorize our role and perform it over and over again. If we get good enough at the role, we're assigned to manage junior associates who play that same role. When we further our education, it is most often with a very specific skill, like database certification, Ajax coding or macchiato making. These are crewing skills, not sailing skills. It's not that crewing skills are bad, or wasted – they are essential. But they are just one iota of what it takes to be the captain of your own boat and guide it through the storm-tossed seas you will inevitably encounter on the course ahead.

When we crew, we go where the boat takes us. When we sail, the boat takes us where we want to go. In the Networked World, we sail on uncharted seas, encountering business scenarios we've never faced before. The more roles we're capable of playing, the more prepared we are to roll with the waves in the market, the better we'll sail.

A third point of clarity: *Improvisation is communication.*

The most vital business skills in the Networked World will not be operational, but communicative. The various operational tasks required for an organization's infrastructure – manufacturing, shipping, payroll, call centers, market analysis, etc. – are becoming ever-more-commoditized as software becomes more sophisticated and new labor pools get wired all around the world. Operational skills are crewing skills. In the Networked World, the valuable skills – the *sailing skills* – will be tied to our ability to communicate. In other words, our ultimate financial success will not be determined by the quality of our manufacturing plant in Kinshasa (excellent though it will be) but by how the brand manufactured in Kinshasa communicates with the marketplace. Or how we ourselves communicate with the marketplace.

Today, we are all living in our own thousand-channel worlds. Business opportunities arise when your thousand-channel world and mine intersect, because that is how information moves, a googol times a googol times per day. Whenever information moves, however micro the transaction, someone makes money. To transact successfully in this new business environment – to move information productively through a network that consists of both people and machines, a network that is both face-to-face and invisible to the eye – we have to communicate well.

Communication has always been the mother's milk of business. Today, organizations that communicate best, both internally and with the marketplace, give themselves the most opportunities for success. The *GameChangers* communication skills touch on all the following aspects of business communication, and more:

- the speed with which work gets done
- sense of purpose
- economy and efficiency of action
- the bonds between your brand and the market
- HR issues
- brainstorming and creativity;
- and of course, communication is a major ingredient in what keeps you in business week-to-week – SALES!

The fourth point: *Improvisation is the human face of business.*

Improvisation consists of an incredible suite of interpersonal communication tools for working at the top of your intelligence as part of a team. Whether it's comedy theater or business, the tools are the same; it is what's being communicated that's different. In both cases, improvisation is the art of being totally in touch with your scene partners, your audience and yourself.

The improviser's range of business skills goes far beyond 'passing along communication', though that's part of it, too. In the hands of a skilled improviser, information gets communicated with emotion and conviction. It explores themes that touch us on a very human level. With everyone living in his or her own thousand-channel info-bubble, skillful, emotional communication will be scarcer than ever before, which makes the ability to communicate with a truly human touch a very important skill to have.

Another point of clarity: *Improvisational success is more than monetary.*

Seeing and experiencing the workaday world through the lens of improvisation is as much about achieving your business and career goals with your lifestyle and integrity intact as it is about making lots of dough. Hey, we all want to make lots of dough. If that's why you're reading this book, rest assured it will help you toward that goal. But if you're like me and you want more; if your definition of success is a professional life integrated with your personal values; if you have the desire to express yourself while working collaboratively within your organization; if you want to move steadfastly in the direction of your dreams while reveling in and being rewarded by every twist and turn along the way, then read on. *GameChangers* was written with you in mind.

The sixth point of clarity: *Improvisation is, first, about you.*

Before there can be organizational growth, there must be individual growth. There's an oft-repeated saying in improv theater, documented by the legendary teacher and author, Mick Napier, in his book, *Improvise: Scene from the Inside Out*: "Take care of yourself first!" Realize that how well your coworkers play along is beyond your control. Here, as Napier describes it, is what's likely to happen if you don't take care of yourself first: "Two people on stage staring at each other and wondering who's going to make the first move. Two people being nice to each other and allowing the other to start doing something. In that short amount of time, two humans have created themselves as powerless." Don't 'create yourself as powerless'. The best thing you can do for yourself is to have a presence, stand for something and engage one hundred percent when you step onto the stage (i.e. arrive for work in the morning). As one of my improv teachers, Jason Pardo, says in his own idiosyncratic way: "Commit! Hang onto your shit!"

Realize that no matter how skillful you are, you will without a doubt be working with people who simply don't want to accept your take on things. They don't have much enthusiasm for working together or for solving problems creatively, and show no interest in building anything new. They are content to remain facilitators and implementers instead of becoming the innovators who bring about new wealth. They cling to the 'tried and true' like barnacles to the hull of a docked ship. Here's another revelation: In business, there *is* no more tried and true. What has been tried is no longer true. And what was true yesterday may not be as true today. You are going to have to be innovative just to keep pace with the changing times. "I always use the metaphor that in old media, you measured everything with a ruler," says Roger Fishman, former president of Fox International, and today president and co-founder of Zizo, a digital media marketing company based in Santa Monica, California. "Today's world is like Silly String. If you imagine taking a can of Silly String and just spraying it, that, to me, is life today. Highly colorful. Highly energetic. Very fluid. And now the question we have to ask ourselves is 'How do we work in a Silly String world?'"

The dogmatic, unimaginative thinkers who can make the workplace such an uninspiring environment have had their day. The future is Now, and Now belongs to the flexible, the free-spirited, the open-minded, the entrepreneurial. It belongs to people with heightened powers of observation who excel in teamwork and creativity. To people who can adapt in a changing business environment. To people who don't *plan* as much as they *prepare*. Who don't *cling*, but *let go*.

"As a corporation, how do we deal with that shift?" asks Zizo's Fishman. "And that's not really a small shift, that's a fundamental shift, which is that you are no longer in control of your destiny. And that is a core challenge and opportunity for organizations."

In the improvisational business model, taking care of yourself first is a fundamental step toward being able to meet the challenges and seize the opportunities Fishman and other entrepreneurs envision. And there's this: As employees raised (educated?) on video games enter the workforce in increasing numbers, the non-linear improvisational skills inherent in the gaming world will naturally become part of the 'Gen-Why?' business culture.

The final point of clarity is this: *When the game changes, GameChangers have the advantage.*

The single biggest business reason that it's important for you to read and understand the concepts in this book is that they can make you a GameChanger. These pages offer a complete set of tools for adapting to change and the practical techniques for using those tools in business.

Change is 'a comin', boys and girls, oh yes it is. Faster than it ever has before. Take just a minute to make a mental list of the way the world has changed in the past ten years alone. Airplane tickets, insurance policies and x-rays are databased and managed in India. Manufacturing jobs have gone to China. You can make phone calls overseas from the dashboard of your car. Animated films are composed in computers. Robots hold down factory jobs once performed by humans. The lettuce in your dinner salad is grown in Guatemala. How many channels could you get on your television when you were in high school, and how many do you get today? Then there's the advent of the internet, with its online commerce, communications, education, banking, social networking, gaming, research, news syndication, blogging and entertainment. And here's the mind-blower: We are in the *primitive stage* of this evolution! The real change is just beginning. As it happens, it will affect the way we live and do business more profoundly than anything since the dawn of the Industrial Revolution.

With the game changing the way it is today, improved improvisational skills will help you see and understand that changing game. "Business *is* the art of improvisation," says Jane Kleinberger, Chairman of the Board and co-founder of Paciolan, a sports and entertainment ticketing company based in Irvine, California, that's a leading innovator in its field. "Every performance you give is unique. It's never completed. The commerce and technology are constantly evolving. What's the value to customers and what does that look like? That changes, too. It's never fixed in place or time. The business is always moving, always evolving, always adapting. It's a work of art in progress."

GameChangers will help you play by the new rules and change the game when the opportunity presents itself. There is a ton of punditry about managing and planning for change. Improvisation gives you the tools to *prepare* for and *participate* in change, and make that experience an enjoyable and profitable one.

THE NETWORKED WORLD

TODAY, A GENERATION OF NEW ORGANIZATIONS like Google, TomTom, Ikea and Microsoft, and established brands like Procter & Gamble, Toyota and the National Basketball Association set new standards for communications in the conduct of business. Many of the successful brands of this emerging era encourage improvisation on an institutional scale. What is Microsoft but the offspring of an early improvisational move made by two players – Bill Gates and Paul Allen – in response to a market opportunity afforded them by IBM? When Jim Stengel, the Chief Marketing Officer of Procter & Gamble, as one of his first moves upon taking the office in 2001, banned storyboards from initial meetings with ad agencies, what filled this fresh vacuum? Improvisation.

The fluid business environment in which these bold moves have taken place and paid off is what I call the *Networked World*. It is an environment whose every electron has been well-documented in publications like *Wired* and *Fast Company*; an environment defined by a Great Pyramid's worth of books, at the top of which sit tomes like Daniel Pink's *A Whole New Mind* and Yochai Benkler's *The Wealth of Networks*; an environment made possible and fueled by internet resources from Amazon to ZeFrank.com. I cannot offer more than what is already known about this environment beyond a view through the very personal prism of my own exploration and experience, which I will bring into focus whenever it's appropriate. More importantly, I offer here a working definition of this world as a 'stomping ground' for the improvisational business and businessperson:

The Networked World is the highly communicative, internet-supported stage on which business gets conducted. It is marked by an unprecedented fluidity and openness of human communications on a global scale. It operates on an unlimited number of channels that are, paradoxically, both highly personalized and depersonalizing.

The Networked World began forming in the mid-1970s to early 1980s, when the forerunners of the internet-organizing brands like Microsoft and Oracle were conceived, and when computer-generated products like *Pac-Man* and *TRON* began to hit the market. It marks the end of the Industrial Age that began with the mass production of manufactured goods in the mid-1800s.

My friend, Richard Taylor, a visual effects director on *TRON*, used to say of the circa-1982 personal computers (Wangs, Kaypros, Ataris, et al) of that era, "We're driving Model T's. You have to know how the engine works just to be able get to Grandma's house and back. Someday, we'll have computers that are like today's cars. You won't have to know how the engine works to drive one. And when that happens, and we can focus on where the car's going, driving is going to be a *lot* more fun." The day predicted by Taylor has arrived. The communications technology that characterizes the Networked World offers unprecedented opportunities for people to get where they want to go in the world. We, each individually, have at our command the ability to knock on and open more doors than all of our ancestors in all of their business ventures combined. The questions we must answer: What doors will we walk through? And how prepared are we for what's on the other side? Improvisation gives us confidence in our choice of doors because we know we're prepared for the opportunity – or challenge – awaiting us on the other side of any of them.

The Industrial Age

Before we further explore the fluid, improvisational model that thrives in the Networked World, let's look at jobs and organizations of the Industrial Age, when standardization and solidity were the bulwarks of the business culture.

Rigid organizations with employees performing meticulously defined and specialized roles mirrored the way the machines of the age operated. A man on an assembly line at the Ford Motor Company's Highland Park plant in 1920s Detroit and a spark plug in a Ford Model-T automobile were both, to the company's way of thinking, duplicable and replaceable. The line kept moving, the machines cranked on, and people and parts got fed to them like fodder for fire.

Standardization became a key element of a company's scalability and success. Mass-produced product proved affordable to mass markets. The predictable supply of products and faster, more reliable forms of transportation followed the channels of telephone, radio and, eventually, television into nearly every home in America. The modes of transportation by which product got shipped, the distribution channels they traveled and the media channels by which they were marketed became part of the mass production machine, too.

Choreographing every little move made by their retail employees and their suppliers brought massive scalability and success to the McDonald's hamburger chain. Without first breaking down the individual production tasks needed to produce a feature-length animated film and assigning them to specialists (story artists, writers, inkers, painters, in-betweeners, clean-up artists, background artists, animators), Walt Disney could never have achieved the stunning production quality that characterized his company's animated films. Nearly all of Hollywood's motion picture factories were exactly that – factories. They churned out images and sound on celluloid with the same assembly line mentality that characterized most manufacturing of the era. Ingénues, leading men, dancers, makeup artists, editors and cinematographers all 'belonged' to the studio, and were shunted through the production process with all the consideration given to car parts on the Ford line.

Empires arose on these industrial structures and created great wealth for a generation of players, but we find ourselves burdened by the structures today, chiefly because we don't live in an age of machines any more. We live in an age of information and communication. Sure, machines are more amazing than they've ever been, and specialization is necessary to complete any kind of complex task, but the problem with rigid organizations is that they build walls between specialists. The tasks performed by the specialists have grown so specialized as to be out of touch with one another. The people who perform them are seldom given the chance to communicate, meaning that ideas within the old-school organization cannot cross-pollinate. Also, many of these structures have grown so strangely Byzantine as to be unmanageable. Industrial Age organizational structures have eroded over time and, in the Networked World, have grown useless and obsolete. And our machines? The more independent and intelligent they get, the more we ask them to mediate business operations as our proxies, the more apparent the need for organizations with a human touch.

Walt Disney began his career as an artist. In that sense, while he was alive, the company never lost touch with its roots. The same was true at Kentucky Fried Chicken, where its founder, Colonel Harlan Sanders, could talk your ear off about how to properly prepare a chicken dinner. After their founders' departures, non-entrepreneurial managers nestled into these empires. The gulf between those allowed by the organization to tread on the sacred grounds of creativity, design, storytelling, branding, innovation, transformation, architecture, fried chicken recipes...and those who were simply executing repetitively, unthinkingly, on the tightly scripted game plan, grew ever wider.

Who was Ebenezer Butterick? He invented the paper dress pattern. Generations of women never bothered with originality again. Instead, they specialized as seamstresses for Butterick's tightly scripted designs. The gap between dressmaking and dress designing grew as a result.

In the melting pot of twentieth century America, standardization had lots of upside. Machines and the products they made offered convincing evidence of our ability to work, play and live together. Television, the greatest one-to-many medium the world had ever seen, reinforced our newly egalitarian society – you ate Kellogg's Frosted Flakes for breakfast, did a bad-ass Tony the Tiger impression ("They're grrrrrrr-eat!") and so did everyone else. And standardization *did* raise living standards, in the vast middle-ground of society anyway. How many housewives stitched better with Butterick's patterns than if they'd tried designing dress patterns their own? How many people who couldn't afford them before bought Ford cars thanks to the assembly lines in Detroit (and to the assembly lines on which they themselves toiled for other industries)?

How many more cakes rose in how many more ovens thanks to the Betty Crocker cake mix and Tappan range factories? Lots. And then... things began to change.

Forces of Nature

The old models are giving way today as surely as mountains succumb to the elements. The citadels of the Industrial Age will either collapse or evolve in wave after wave of change brought on by the global digital economy. The Networked World demands a fluid model, one that can roll with those waves of change. A new, more flexible and creative type of business organization has become inexorably necessary and ultimately unavoidable. This new business structure will accommodate new ways of working and new generations of employees doing that work. This new structure is *the network*. The networked organization communicates, both internally and with the world, via a massive, ever-changing constellation of channels. It is increasingly non-hierarchical. It provides fertile territory for those businesspeople with entrepreneurial instincts, no matter where they reside in the organizational scheme of things.

Just as in the Industrial Age, the organizations of the Networked World mirror the way products get produced. The way products get produced today is via networks. These networks enable the complex web of communication required to connect production lines that may run all the way from Kokomo to Kinshasa; and they open the endless matrix of marketing, sales and distribution points made possible by the internet. The effectiveness of a company's performance in this wonderfully chaotic networked environment will ultimately decide the success of the business.

Organizations designed to thrive in the Networked World are more *biological* than industrial. They resemble their employees more than their employees resemble them. They are highly adaptive, open, sensitive to their culture and their environment, and ultra-responsive to their audience. They continuously evolve, nurtured by a steady stream of intelligent input from inside *and* outside the organizational organism. In this biological archetype, *where* good ideas originate is not half as important as *how* those good ideas are nurtured toward realization and profitability.

Compare the Industrial Age Ford production line described

earlier with an automobile factory of the Networked World – Toyota's Tsutsumi plant at its manufacturing complex in Toyota City, Japan. On this plant's 'improvisational' production lines, every single car is custom-built to order with Just-In-Time (JIT) inventory – only two hours worth of parts stored on the manufacturing floor at any one time. Employees on the line know what model of automobile is coming down the line by the music that accompanies it. If there's any kind of snag in the process, a worker pulls a dangling white 'andon cord' prompting a different piece of music, upon which the anomaly gets smoothly re-routed back up the line for fixing. Managers at the plant spend most of their time tending to the robots; the people manage themselves on this highly flexible and adaptive system. Toyota claims that of the 600,000 suggestions made by employees at their Toyota City facility in 2005 (an average of more than one suggestion a month by every employee) 95% got implemented. In this model, the improvisational manufacturing model, work consists of a fluid process that honors suggestions, adapts to unexpected situations that come up in the course of a scene, and harnesses both the collaborative power of the group and the contributions of its individual members. And all of it is focused on a specific business objective, the production of high-quality hybrid cars.

My first glimpse into the Networked World came when I worked as the staff publicist on *TRON*, in 1982. But that was crude work on primitive computers plugged into 300-baud phone lines. We willed ourselves, wired ourselves, into a future that had not yet arrived. It was a dozen years later, when I produced the web site for the film *Toy Story* in 1994 that I truly experienced the way the Networked World works.

An online neophyte at the time, I'd recently given a very dramatic presentation about the new digital media to 30 people in Disney's film marketing division (a photo editor broke into tears when I predicted that the photographic records of a feature film would be far more public in the future, and that the job of the photo editor would be to *create* access, not *limit* it. "That's…not…what we *do*!" she sniffled). Two fearless and far-sighted Disney executives, Brett Dicker and Kellie Allred, subsequently hired me to produce the *Toy Story* site when I convinced them the film was a perfect fit for the internet audience. The site, designed by Canto 5 Productions and programmed by Two-

Lane Media, turned out magnificently. It was easily the best movie web site that had ever been done to that time. My favorite feature was *Bo Peep's Advice for Toys*, an online column written by a precocious 12-year-old, Hillary Ellenshaw, in which different toys would 'write to Bo' for relationship advice and personal counseling.

Imagine my mortification when I began receiving unsolicited emails from employees of Pixar, suggesting 'fixes' for the site. Dozens of them. Everything from versioning problems to improper text alignment. We quickly went to work addressing the fixes, but this, I thought, was a disaster in the making. A revolt by Pixar against work done by Disney, or some such thing. "Brett Dicker and Kellie Allred are going to get a phone call from (*Toy Story* Directory John) Lasseter any minute," I thought. "And that'll be that. I'm done."

Maybe it would have happened that way in the Industrial Age. But this was the dawn of the Networked World. The emails from Pixar were not a signal of condemnation but of *support!* They were pitching in to help get the job done! Once I realized this, the work took on even more luster. ToyStory.com became the first URL ever featured as part of a movie marketing campaign. At its zenith, it was getting over three million 'hits' (metric of the time) a day. For me, it signaled that business in the future would not get done the same way it had gotten done in the past. This future would get built by people with common interests working collaboratively for the good of the group. There would be no blueprint for this evolution. No script. Its creators would improvise it into existence.

II. THE HOUR OF PLAY

You can discover more about a person
in an hour of play than in a year of conversation.

— *Plato*

SCENES

IN THE PARLANCE OF *GAMECHANGERS*, every encounter between two or more players who share a business-related objective is a *Scene*. In business, all the Networked World's a stage and you cannot afford to be a poor player upon it. Meetings, panel discussions, reviews, interviews, hirings, firings, hearings, testimonials, drinks, meals, plane flights, cab rides, train trips, receptions, parties, whiteboarding sessions, retreats, IMs, phone calls, videoconferences, reviews, break room gatherings, and chance elevator encounters are all settings in which business scenes take place. By treating them as improvised scenes, you will be able to assess them in terms of their effectiveness at reaching their objectives, just like improv theater performers do. The criteria for critiquing improvised scenes are well established. You can use these criteria as a lens through which everything you and your teammates do in business can be viewed. By looking at scenes through this lens, you (or your coach) can critique performances by individuals and groups without stepping on anyone's ego or personal ambitions. In *GameChangers*, everyone's ambition is the same – to become a better improviser. We work at different jobs, toward different goals, but the improvisation techniques used by those at the top of every trade are the same. And so are the criteria by which those techniques are judged.

Before we get too far into how to determine the effectiveness of scenes, we need to delve a little deeper into the definition of a scene as it relates to business. It's not as simple as a scene in improv theater. In a theater performance, two or more players step onstage, establish the 'Who, What and Where' of the characters, reveal the objective, and then spend a couple of minutes performing toward that objective, coincidentally utilizing elements such as conflict and exaggeration to generate laughs. When it has run its course, the scene either gets edited and a new scene begins or the lights black out, ending the show.

Parallels and Differences

Business scenes have parallels with improv theater scenes, as well as differences. First, the parallels…

Like improv theater scenes, *business scenes involve a cast of characters.* The motivations of these characters and their relationships with one another can be more complex than anything on an improv stage.

Think of the teams with whom you work: What are the personalities of the members? What roles do they play in your scenes? What is their status within the group? How do the players on your teams relate to one another? What is your team chemistry? Of each person with whom you work, consider these questions: What is the essence of their character? What motivates them? What relationships are most important in their lives? How do they see themselves? What emotions do they use to communicate? Question, questions… the answers different for every character and every team. All teams and their players operate within their own reality, consisting of the experiences (life, work, spiritual), education and genetics that have shaped and defined them from conception to the present. Only when these realities have been acknowledged, agreed to, and to some degree understood by all the players in the group, can a business scene realize its full potential.

Like improv scenes, *business scenes are intended to explore the objective.* It is not hard to imagine what some typical business-related objectives might be. Product design. A budget. A merger. An ad campaign. A launch. Sales. Think back on the meetings/scenes you've had over the past week. What was the objective? Was it clear? Was it shared by your scene partners? Was your team focused on it? Sometimes the shortcoming of a scene is that the objective is not clear to all the players in the scene, resulting in a lack of focus. A worthy objective, one which the players in the group share an interest, if not an emotional stake, is a prerequisite for a good scene. (For more on objectives and why they are important, see the *Coaching* chapter.)

Finally, like improv scenes, *business scenes exist to please the audience.* As you can imagine, the audience for a business scene is not simply 'those people sitting in the seats out there in the dark whose approval you seek'. The definition of the business audience begins with the fact that *sometimes the audience is not physically present for a scene.* She may be a single mother from Cleveland who's in the market for learning toys for her child and she does not even know you're having your product design scene back at Totzot Ltd. while you're having it. But if it's a productive scene, she will eventually respond by buying Totzot's products. And so will thousands of others like her in the Totzot audience. Their applause comes in the form of demand and sales. If you improvise well in business, *you* are the one laughing.

A business performance gets judged by both *external* and *internal* audiences; that is, those outside the company and those within it. The external audience includes customers (the audience that matters most), competitors, the government, media, and other constituencies one must please or reckon with if one is in business. Internal audiences consist primarily of employees or close associates of your company who screen ideas, offer direction and, in some cases, have veto power before a business performance goes public. Borrowing a phrase from the film business, I call this the *screening audience.* This gauntlet of opinionators sitting like *American Idol* judges between your brand and your public includes coworkers, management, boards of directors, investors, suppliers, analysts, your spouse and your highly opinionated children. Players should be as considerate and 'on' as possible for all audiences, but ultimately *it is the customer audience that determines the fate of your brand.* It is possible to fail in business while pleasing your customer audience. But it is not possible to succeed if you fail them. Even if you're one of those businesspeople who makes a career of hornswoggling investors, the customer audience (in this case, naive investors) must be pleased long enough for you to cash out in the middle of the night the way you do.

More differences between improvising for yuks and improvising for bucks…

Unlike improv theater scenes, business scenes have no particular duration and can be continued over intervals of time. Some scenes, a weekly staff meeting for example, might go on for weeks or even years. Others can be brief one-time encounters. As long as the objective does not change and the players involved do not change their roles, a scene as defined in the context of business can go on indefinitely. Performances by great brands can run longer than any theatrical show in history. Great brands, as they say in showbiz, have legs.

Compared to improv theater, the *cast of characters in a business scene can be huge*. It's nothing to have dozens or even hundreds of players interacting in a scene. And scenes in business can be virtual. Not only does the audience not have to be there, the players themselves don't have to be there. The cast can be scattered around the globe. It's still a scene. It has a Who-What-Where (even if the Where is cyberspace). It has a cast of characters. It has an objective. It's a scene. In business, if the objective is broad enough, as in a company-wide greening campaign, the cast can consist of every employee of the company. For a Fortune 500 company, that can mean 50,000 people all theoretically in the same scene.

Another important distinction of business scenes: *A person can be both player and audience*. The most frequent example of this is a sales scene, in which the player representing the brand interacts with a potential customer who is a partner in the scene and is also the determiner of the scene's fate. Will the scene result in a sale? That's something only the audience can decide. Another typical business scene in which a performer can also be the audience is one where a hands-on manager, or some other person responsible for coaching a team, participates fully in the give-and-take of the scene, and then 'gives notes' on the scene. Other managers, who are not as hands-on, prefer to remain in the role of coach, guiding the scene, side-coaching and critiquing. That's valid, too. Either way, business decisions must be made, directions chosen and actions taken. Someone has to do that. It's entirely possible that the person doing it is one of your scene partners.

Obviously, the purpose of most business scenes is not to get laughs or television ratings. The purpose of improvisational business scenes is to conduct business effectively in the Networked World. This is a serious, too often all-consuming undertaking. It requires life balancing, keen instincts, reaction speed, communication skills and focus – all of which happen to be the hallmarks of good improvisers. The audience may respond in different ways and at wildly different intervals, depending on the business you're in. But if they *do* respond, the payoff, as in improv theater, is a happy reaction along with the effect their reaction has on revenue.

Evaluating Scenes

The most important question improv performers ask themselves after a performance is just as important, and therefore valid, for judging business scenes: *How well did we move toward the objective?* When a scene works improvisationally, when it moves well toward its objective, there are a multitude of elements that have factored into its success. The entire contents of this book could be funneled into any scene as fuel. Skilled improvisers possess the entire repertoire.

Good scenes engage us from the instant they begin. We understand the characters involved, relate to them and know what makes them tick. Good scenes move, not only in the all-important sense of being physically active and energetically alive, but also in the sense of constantly moving toward the objective. A team of improvisers does not know how a scene will resolve, but plays resolutely, with confidence and direction. Movement toward the objective brings focus, gracefulness, clarity and life to a scene. When players move as a group toward the objective, we, as the audience, move with them. This movement carries us, players and audience alike, to the transcendent place where new understandings arise and new realities take shape. In business, the new realities are the ever-evolving attributes of your brand. The audience doesn't see the thousands of moves you make every day within your company, but it does see and respond to the evolution of your brand in the marketplace.

Here are a few other hallmarks of good scenes, and why they're important:

Good scenes have good energy. The energy with which a group performs is infectious and speaks unambiguously to the audience. It is both a sign of professionalism and respect for the audience that you perform with good energy. It indicates that you're engaged in the scene. It says that members of your team are connected and working well together. This good energy does not have to be high-pitched. Who wants to be in scene after scene in which people are jumping on the furniture? That will burn you out in no time. Quiet, low-key scenes can have good energy if that energy is focused on the objective.

Good scenes resonate emotionally. The most profound form of communication is emotional. Scenes often rise or fall based on the emotional involvement of the players. Emotion guarantees energy. It indicates involvement. It is what causes the audience to sit up in its seats, eager to see where a scene will take them. My parents' Happy Days Generation had a word for the kind of emotion it takes to get a business scene really going: *gumption*! If you had gumption, you had the guts to stand for your convictions and you backed them with action. If you had gumption, you put your professional pride on the line. You were an optimist. Today, many organizations, caught in the switches between Industrial Age and Networked World, suffer from a gumption shortage. They strive for certainty where there is none. The emotions of players in these organizations are often fear-based, and range from paralyzing caution to out-and-out pessimism about the future. Extreme, hysterical or negative emotions don't do much good in our day-to-day working lives, where common sense and practical, reasoned decision-making must prevail. Bringing hysteria to a business scene is like playing chess while wearing boxing gloves. You can try to make a move but all you do is knock down a lot of other players. Business requires more nuanced and upbeat emotions.

The last vestiges of Industrial Age behavior in business are saturated with negativity – and why shouldn't they be? These behaviors are *dying* – we can't expect happiness and dancing around a deathbed, can we? Fraught as they are with paranoia, denial, secrecy, scarcity, command, control and subterfuge, these behaviors weigh down a scene and stand between it and its objective. The environment that is most receptive to business in the Networked World also happens to be hospitable to improvisers. The behaviors that characterize good scenes radiate with positive, productive emotions: optimism, patience, passion, pride of ownership, persistence, industriousness, confidence, respect…you know, *gumption*.

Good scenes explore relationships. Your business consists of a mosaic of relationships: your relationship with your scene partners, your brand's relationship with your audience, your audience's relationships with one another. Business, when you get down to the fundamentals, is about relationships between people. Millions can change hands without any kind of contract ever being signed based solely on the relationships between characters in a scene. Sales depend on the relationship between seller and buyer, and between buyer and brand. Productive collaborations depend on the working relationships between players.

In the Networked World, we take our technology for granted. We're wired. Some of us are super-wired. When it comes to business, to be unwired is unwise, because it means missing out on transactions of information that sustain every business. Super-wiring does not, however, guarantee a super scene. Technology is not a relationship. Effective scenes are about relationships between people. Technology is the plumbing of the networked business. Relationships are the water that fills the pipes and sustains the life within.

Sometimes scenes suck. It's a fact of life, one that improvisers accept and learn from. We have all been in bad scenes. They are inevitable, just as even great golfers hit a bad shot on occasion. The difference between pros and hacks is that the pros hit far fewer bad shots. The same is true with improvisation. Good improvisers appear in far fewer bad scenes. And just as the best in the game of golf are adept at recovering from a bad shot brilliantly, the best teams can salvage practically any situation and turn apparent mistakes into gold.

You can't avoid trouble – when you're in it, you're in it. But you can avoid areas that lead to trouble. Just as a great golfer will shape a shot to steer it away from hazards on the course, agile improvisers help keep a scene away from what they know to be potential performance problems. They do it by focusing on what they know to be productive. There are an uncountable number of productive moves in the repertoire of the skilled improviser. One of the most reliable moves is to support your fellow players. This is a not only a good move for business purposes, but for living your life as well.

GAMES

ASK YOURSELF THIS QUESTION: Would you rather work or play? The answer is easy. If we could afford to, just about all of us would choose play over work because play, by definition, is much more fun. Playing (unless your idea of play is competitive eating, hydroplane racing, bounty hunting or some combination of the three) relieves stress, improves your mental and physical health, and fills you with good energy.

Let's pose the possibility that, through improvisation, *work can take on the qualities of play.* Imagine that you're not going to work any more. You're going to play! We are not glossing over the fundamental facts of business life here. Serious work must get done. Products packaged and shipped on time. Forms completed. Satellites launched. Stalls mucked. Fires put out. But how much more exciting would work be if it happened within the context of a game being played, with you as one of the game's primo players?

History and Theory

Modern improv theory began with the playing of *Games*. In the 1920s, Neva Boyd, a Northwestern University professor in sociology, and her protégé, Viola Spolin, used simple games to help immigrant children of many different nationalities on Chicago's South Side communicate and assimilate into their new culture. Spolin's son, Paul Sills, would later co-originate Second City, where he and his performers used his mother's foundational work with games to perform improvised comedy. It was Spolin who observed that a fundamental transformation took place during the playing of group games. At the heart of this transformation is something akin to spiritual transcendence – the setting aside of oneself and one's ego for a higher purpose. When a game is played, all of a sudden it's not about you or me. It's about us. And because it's about us – not about an individual, but about the activity of a group – the playing of games generates an experience that is engaging, not only to the players, but for the audience as well.

For this book, I define games as *group activities undertaken for the purpose of achieving an objective*. It is apparent that this definition describes business every bit as well as it describes theater or sport. Games are the glue that hold improvised scenes together. Their rules, the teamwork they engender and the objective they define hold the group's focus and bring about the group mind.

Skilled improvisers perceive and play games on *three levels*. First, they recognize the game being played and are quick to grasp its rules. In business, this means that you can read people quickly and understand group dynamics. Second, they have the knowledge and skill to participate fully in the game. In business, this means expertise in your field and commitment to your job. Third, improvisers understand the importance of the game in the larger world. In business, this means you understand how your actions as an employee support the larger mission of the organization.

Just as games would become Viola Spolin's building blocks for a new kind of theatrical technique, they can be your building blocks for a new approach to work. Think of it as 'business-as-theater'. In this approach, your business performance is composed of a series of scenes, and games are the stuff those scenes are built on. With an understanding of games, you'll be able to look at every business encounter in a completely different way.

One of the first things to understand about improvisation games is that *there are no winners or losers*. There are only players or bystanders. You either see the game or you don't. You are either in the game or you're not. You either have the skills to play or you need to acquire them, and until then, all you can do is stand in the wings and watch the pros do their thing. Just because there are no winners and losers doesn't mean, however, that there's no outcome. Businesspeople need and expect outcomes that are measured in a million different ways – revenues, stock price, margins, sales quotas, quality assurance, milestones, delivery dates, you name it. Outcomes are of paramount importance. It's also important to understand that games are what drive scenes toward an outcome. These are not games with point spreads, victors and the vanquished. There is only the shared drive by your team toward a desired outcome. When a satisfactory outcome is achieved, when the objective is met, all win.

How Games Are Played

Okay, enough about history and theory. Let's get down to the nitty-gritty of playing the game. How, in the context of business does one go about playing a game?

In every business scenario, there's an opportunity to play a game. This does not mean there's going to be a game played in every scenario. Generally, however, a scene does not come to life or have any break-through potential unless a game is played. The difference between a scene with a game and one without is the difference between making soup and boiling water. In order for a scene to have a chance to work improvisationally, players must agree to play a game. And before it can be played, the game must be identified.

A typical business game that everyone knows well and can identify easily without any training is commonly called 'Kissing Ass'. There are more productive and useful games, of course. I'm only using this as an example because everyone's familiar with it, not because I advocate playing it. In this scenario, players spot the game when the highest status person in a meeting throws out a really lame, impractical idea and you or a coworker labels it as pure genius and the highest status person agrees. And there you have it – game on. That game will almost definitely drive the scene from that point onward. No matter what you do to change or divert it, you're stuck with it, even if the rest of the meeting plays out like a month of *Dilbert* cartoon strips. *Games begin when an activity tied to an objective is acknowledged and agreed to by the group.* The game of Kissing Ass did not begin until the highest status person acknowledged and accepted the ass-kissing. At that point, there is an activity (praising lame ideas) tied to an objective (currying favor with the boss), and the game is underway. A lot of ground can be covered in the aforementioned meeting, but the game will never stray far from Kissing Ass.

Just because a game gets played, there's no guarantee it's going to be a particularly productive or well-played one. But more experienced improvisers can spot and find consensus on the good ones right away. That's why it's ultra-important to recognize games in business. Not only does being an adept business improviser enable you to spot the game, it lets you see the many possibilities for different games within a scene. It lets you choose productive games over unproductive ones.

If I'm interviewing for a job, the interviewer and I are probably going to play a game. It may be as simple as a straightforward and familiar game called 'Job Interview', in which the most noteworthy occurrence in the scene is the pro forma initiation by the interviewer, "Tell me why you're the right person for this job." At that point, it's up to me to make the game as interesting and compelling as possible for the audience (the interviewer and unseen others who are not in the room but whom I'm trying to impress). Or there could be a subtler game being played, such as 'Final Jeopardy', in which the entire selection process comes down to a single issue of salary, experience or willingness to relocate. If I'm still talking about why I'm the best person for the job, but the game is Final Jeopardy, I'm probably going to tank the interview. A savvy player sees the multiple games that could be played and plays the most productive one.

"We had a project manager resign to take a less stressful job," says David LaPlante, CEO of Twelve Horses, Inc., an internet consulting and production company in Reno, Nevada. "My first thought was to replace her with the most skilled, hard-assed project management person I could find. Obvious, right? But when I looked at the situation, I realized that the project manager who'd resigned was a major influencer of company opinion. I counted on her to build consensus for our business objectives. The game we needed to play was not 'Replace the Project Manager', but 'Replace the Opinion-Shaper'. This meant that, against the advice of our lawyers, I stayed in touch with the outgoing project manager, and got her to help me recruit her replacement. Because she'd been an influence on our staff, this helped build confidence in the transition and led us to hire a replacement whose people skills were as strong as his ability to manage projects. I never look at any business situation any more without asking myself, 'What's the game?'"

What happens if you attempt to change the game mid-scene? Or play more than one game in a scene? More than likely, chaos will ensue and the scene will careen wildly like a rocket with a bad gyroscope. *In general,* games are too fragile, subtle and embedded in the subtext of a scene to get discarded and have new ones begun while the scene is in motion. Abandoning a game results in disagreement, confusion and the need for follow-up clarification later on. Once you have begun a game, you're almost always saddled with it for the duration of a scene, sometimes for the duration of a business campaign or working relationship.

Scene: Here's an example of two people who played a game for nearly their entire working relationship. One day, when one of them decided to unexpectedly change the game, it ended the relationship. Michael Eisner and Jeffrey Katzenberg had a solid working relationship for over 20 years. As a protégé to Eisner and Barry Diller, Katzenberg learned his trade at Paramount Pictures from two of the most powerful and successful executives in the entertainment business. When Eisner left Paramount to become the CEO and Chairman of The Walt Disney Company, Katzenberg went with him as head of production at Walt Disney Studios. Although Eisner was still his boss, Katzenberg had one of the most powerful jobs in entertainment, with oversight of hundreds of millions in development and production budgets, management of the studio's vital relationships with top talent, and the business goal of revitalizing the Disney's moribund feature film division in the eyes of Hollywood and the world.

The complex relationship between Eisner and Katzenberg had always been based on a simple game: Katzenberg, with his seemingly boundless drive and energy, kept his fingers on the pulse of the business and reported everything back to Eisner, who would, with Katzenberg's input, make strategic business decisions. It was known in the entertainment trade as the 'Golden Retriever' game, and it worked beautifully for the duo during their early years at Disney. They lured major stars and filmmakers to Disney projects, built new brands, opened new markets for the studio's live-action films, and lit a wildly productive fire under the Disney Animation department, which turned out modern classics like *The Little Mermaid* and *The*

Lion King. And then, a tragic accident disrupted the balance of power at Disney, the game changed, and the Eisner-Katzenberg relationship got very publicly shredded because of it.

On Sunday, April 3, 1994, Frank Wells, President of Disney, Eisner's counterpart at the top of the management mountain, and an avid climber and skier of real mountains, died in a helicopter crash while on a skiing vacation in Utah. The next morning, without informing Eisner, Katzenberg accessed Wells' business calendar and appeared at meetings Wells had been scheduled to attend. In other words, Katzenberg changed the game without telling his longtime scene partner, Eisner. From that point on, things went south in a hurry. Furious that Katzenberg assumed Wells' role without discussing it with him first, Eisner not only didn't hand over the company presidency that Katzenberg assumed would be rightfully his, he froze any attempts by Katzenberg to take on more responsibility within the company. It put a chill on their relationship that never thawed, later resulting in a very nasty public lawsuit and trial. Katzenberg walked away with a partnership with Steven Spielberg and David Geffen in the new DreamWorks Studios, and was later awarded $200 million in his wrongful termination suit against Disney. For the remaining 11 years of Eisner's tenure as CEO, the job of President of The Walt Disney Company remained unfilled. I guess the moral of the story is that if you're going to change the game and lose your job because of it, make sure the next game you play is called 'Spielberg and the Golden Parachute'.

Bad Games

Games are the building blocks of scenes, but they do not predict the outcome of a scene any more than our DNA code predicts what we're having for lunch tomorrow. The outcome is up to the players. That said, there are some games that make it nearly impossible for the group to achieve its objective in a scene. One of the biggest shortcomings for aspiring entrepreneurs and managers is that they get stuck playing games that are not as productive as other games would be. Here are some classically unproductive games played every day in businesses around the world:

Buffing and Turfing. This game got named by Samuel Shem, author of the classic hospital novel, *House of God*. Buffing and Turfing is the game played when someone comes to you with a problem and you don't want it to be your problem, but don't want to offend them or seem unhelpful, either. So you Buff the problem by improving it cosmetically with minimal effort ("I made some phone calls...") and then Turf it by sending the person with the problem looking elsewhere ("Here's who *I* think you should call...") for help. Variations of this game are 'Good Luck With That' and 'I'd Love To But I'm Swamped'.

Playing Stupid. Thanks to my friend, Harrison Ellenshaw, for pointing this one out to me. "The highest ranking executive in the room gets to ask the dumbest questions," Harrison explains. "It's a rule." While I don't agree that it's a hard-and-fast rule, especially in the creative process, where lots of stupid things get said to highlight the smart ones, Harrison puts his finger on a game that definitely gets played throughout the business universe. Imagine a group of executives looking at a prototype of a new product. Let's say it's a pet-tracking collar. The player who asks, "Will this collar track pets?" – *that's* the highest-ranking executive in the room. The people who initiate this game are like double-agents in the land of the stupid – they really *don't* know a lot about the subject being discussed and to show that they don't know would be a sign of weakness. Their game, therefore, is to play *so* stupid that everyone assumes they really must have some kind of sneaky genius going for them, because no one's *that* stupid. Not only is this game notoriously unproductive while it's being played, it also takes a post-performance toll, as employees devote many water cooler hours and IMs to the story of the exec who wanted to know if the pet-tracking collar on which the company had invested millions was in fact a collar that could track pets. Despite its impediment to productivity, it does take some level of sophistication to Play Stupid, and many high profile careers have been built largely on the ability to play it well. This game goes by many names, including 'Short Attention Span Theater' and 'Still on Tokyo Time'.

Joke Train. This game gets played in meetings where the primary output is laughter. Everyone likes to laugh, and a good laugh line is almost always appreciated in a meeting as long as it doesn't come at anyone's expense, or at least anyone who's in the room. When you take a ride on the joke train, however, it's hard to get off. Pretty soon, everyone gets so preoccupied with looking for things to make fun of, the scene's objective gets left at the station. Everyone comes out of this meeting with a smile, but most of the work still looms and will require an inordinate amount of follow-up and sorting through. And that person you made fun of who was not in the room at the time? You're going to hear from them. Spamming everyone on the company mailing list with the latest YouTube video or anything else that you personally find hilarious (but which others may not) can also fall into the category of playing the 'Joke Train' game.

Here Come Da Judge. Like Playing Stupid, this is another game typically initiated by high status individuals, usually in some kind of review meeting, or where those in attendance are asked for their opinions. The game revolves around who can be the last person in the room to weigh in on a given topic, indicating that their word is the final and therefore most authoritative. Scenes in which this game is played often turn into tense, politically charged situations, with much emphasis placed on individual winners and losers within the group. In the improvisational model, competition within a group is a point of *zero* emphasis. Groups themselves can and should be very competitive, but on behalf of their brand and in the interest of achieving their objectives. Competition within a team leads to non-productive behavior.

That Reminds Me of a Story. Often initiated by more senior players, this one can be a real buzz-kill in any business meeting. Before learning improv, I myself was an egregious initiator of this game. It was easy for me – *everything* reminds me of a story, and I'm good at telling them. I often initiated the game by explaining that every business has a narrative and our job as employees is bringing that narrative to life. True? Maybe. But here's the *pertinent* truth about telling stories in business meetings, a truth I only realized after studying improv: Every time I told a story, the scene I was in would slow to a standstill. Minds wandered. Agendas collapsed. Productivity took a nap. As the deliverer of an extended monologue, I smothered the back-and-forth communications between players that is essential to a productive scene.

Good Games

By contrast, many games played all the time in business have the potential to be hugely productive, and richly rewarding to the group playing them. Golden Retriever, for instance, resulted in ten years of big profits and a total turnaround of The Walt Disney Company's fortunes. Here are some other games with the potential to be productive:

Go Big Or Stay Home (aka GOBOSH). This game works well when initiated in a creatively themed meeting, and can also be effective when initiated by a charismatic company leader. The objective of this game usually revolves around making a big splash with your moves. Market activity around a brand gets churned up by all the splashing that results from GOBOSH. Ted Turner won the America's Cup sailing competition. He bought the Atlanta Braves. Big moves. He conceived of cable news (CNN) as a legitimate medium for major advertisers, and of a superstation (TBS) competitive with the major television networks. Turner went big, and when he finally 'went home' in 2003 when he resigned as Vice-Chairman of Time-Warner, it was for bigger than big money – $784 million from the sale of 60 million shares of Time-Warner stock. Will Richard Branson's Virgin Air ever turn a profit on space travel? Who knows, but it is the sort of wonderfully provocative, never-done-before idea that connects with the public's imagination and communicates the Virgin brand's personality to its audience. When the GOBOSH game has been initiated by a leading personality in an organization, the other players in the organization are emboldened to follow with big moves of their own.

Mutual Interest. Lizzie Widhelm, head of west coast sales for Pandora, a personalized wi-fi radio network, described this game to me. "First, I listen," she says.

"What are you listening for?" I ask.

"Anything my customer and I might have in common. Do we share an interest in music? Is it about sports? The latest music? Do they have young children? Salespeople sometimes get a bad reputation for being slippery. Finding a Mutual Interest is not about being a bullshit artist. I want to find a way for my customers and me to have an honest connection. So I get them to talk, and I listen, and when we find something we honestly have in common, we can begin to form a relationship. They've given me a 'ball' that I can toss back at them, and that's the game – keep that ball going back and forth between you and the customer."

With the game initiated, Widhelm pays close attention to subsequent communication – 'the ball going back and forth' – between her and the sales prospect. "Eventually, the dialogue will be about my product line and their business goals. When the time comes for them to buy, I want to be top of mind. And that can only happen if we keep playing the game. Sometimes it goes on for two years before there's a sale." Widhelm goes on to point out that the sales cycle is different for every business. According to her, what matters is keeping the game, in this case the game of Mutual Interest, alive.

Let's Pretend. Noe Sanchez, a top salesman for Clinique skin care products, who studies and performs at I.O. West, describes a game he plays during a much shorter sales cycle. "When I do skin care and makeup consultations, I have only a couple seconds to get someone's attention, so I initiate an improv scene," says Sanchez. "I let the customer know right away this is going to be something different. People love playing games, so that's what we do – we play a little game."

"Excuse me," he will say to women walking through a department store, "I'm the chief makeup scientist for Clinique. We're conducting experiments here today, and I'm wondering if you'd like to participate."

"People know we're just playing, that I'm not really the chief scientist," Sanchez says. "But it stops people. Gets them to pay attention. The science of makeup, you know, it's not something people normally think about, but they're interested in it.

Continues Sanchez: "A lot of sales consultants start by asking a simple question like 'Would you like to get a makeover today?' And before they've even finished asking, the customer is like, 'Uh, no, thanks. Why should I believe your products are any different from anyone else's?' My job is to help people believe they're going to be more beautiful if they sit in that chair and try the Clinique products. I take a more imaginative approach and it pays off. My bosses at Clinique ask how I do it. They say, 'Noe, what's your secret? We want everybody to have some of that Noe Magic.'" Sanchez shrugs. "No secret. I tell them it's all about the improv."

Crazy Like a Fox. The film director, Tim Burton, is a master of this game. I once watched Burton play the Crazy game in a screening of the dailies for *Cabin Boy*, a film he produced but did not direct, starring the great Chris Elliot. The film was a glorious mess at the time, and everyone in the screening room had ideas for how to improve it. The final word apparently belonged to Jeffrey Katzenberg, Disney's head of production at the time, who was playing Here Come Da Judge by waiting to have the last word. Katzenberg made his comments, upon which everyone got up to leave the screening room. And then Burton, who'd been sitting scrunched down in the front row, said, "Just a second." Everyone sat back down for the new game, which they knew from experience would be enjoyable. It is always interesting to see what's on Burton's mind, and even more interesting to see how he communicates it. The rhythms and modes of expression he uses are completely unique. Burton stood up and started waving his hands, gesturing wildly at the screen.

"Where's the, you know, the good stuff? It was in there. That stuff was funny! The background characters and the, Chris did that thing, you know the thing, and that was so funny but none of it's in here, what it needs, more of that…because it was so great when he…I love that stuff! And…" Burton paused dramatically and turned his heavy-lidded gaze directly on Katzenberg. "Where's the bathroom?" he asked.

The screening room was in the bizarrely designed Team Disney building, so it took a small entourage to help Burton find a bathroom. While the 'Fox' was away, Katzenberg and the others continued the game he had initiated, interpreting just what was behind Burton's craziness. The game Burton and the others play, and someone you know or work with surely plays, too, also goes by 'The Nutty Professor' and 'My Genius is Close to My Madness'. Note that this game is quite similar in its initiation to Playing Stupid, but different in that it is designed to provoke creativity and imaginative thinking on the part of the game's other participants.

As stated earlier, it's best to commit completely to a game and exhaust its possibilities toward achieving the objective. But in business, sometimes a scene must continue even though the possibilities of a game *have* been exhausted. In these instances, it is okay to introduce another, potentially more productive, game to the scene. When Tim Burton changed the game to Crazy Like a Fox, it was in the interest of getting better, more productive ideas out of the group. *When the objective is not achieved by playing a game to its conclusion, change the game.*

Favors. This game is one of the all-time classics. Indeed, some businesspeople maintain that this is the only game that matters, that the very conduct of business itself is defined by the playing of this particular game. It begins with one player extending a favor, usually a small one, to another. The favor either gets re-paid by the second player, thus beginning a relationship based on favors extended and repaid, or the first player repeatedly does favors for the second player until the second player owes a considerable 'debt' that can be repaid in the form of a business transaction. Favors can come in all shapes and sizes. *Work-related favors*, for example, might consist of covering for a fellow employee who needs to leave work early, volunteering to proofread an important document or helping a coworker meet a deadline. *Social favors* are those not directly related to business, including invitations to join country clubs, tickets to concerts or a good table at a special restaurant. These favors often come in the context of mutual interests – you know good wines and so do I – that lead to relationships that in turn lead to business. I know an executive who curried great favor for many years by circulating well-written restaurant reviews to everyone in his business circle. *Hybrid favors* mix business with pleasure. A high-profile example of this kind of favor is investment banker Herbert Allen's annual Sun Valley, Idaho, retreat for major players in the media, entertainment and financial worlds – at which attendees both recreate and play some of the biggest money games in the world of business.

Bucket Brigade. Some of the most energetic and focused business games occur in times of crisis, when something threatens the team or the organization itself. If you have been in business for any time whatsoever, you have played a crisis-inspired game. Bucket Brigade is one variation of the genre. In it, the objective is to help the person 'nearest the fire'. Information, resources, and as many supportive moves as possible get made by the team on behalf of those person or persons taking the most heat. When a team bands together to save someone's job because management doesn't see the value of that member to the team, that's Bucket Brigade. Other business scenarios in which this game might get played: a member of your sales team is in danger of missing a quota; an enterprise server breaks down; or an on-the-job injury. Similar games include 'Holding Down the Fort' and 'Cover Me, I'm Going In'.

At the Wire. A race against the clock. The last push. Everyone focused and on task. Everyone fully present and accountable. This game gets played in climactic scenes, as when your product is ready to launch, a deadline looms, or the road show begins. The ultimate example is a NASA countdown to blastoff. All the facts are on the table, every digit in the sequence is mission-critical, there is zero tolerance for error or omission…billions of dollars, the pride of a nation, the future itself, on the line…in ten….nine….

Players

BECAUSE IMPROV PERFORMANCES ARE BUILT ON THE PLAYING of games, it's only natural that improv performers are known as *Players* and that groups of players are known as teams. In the context of *GameChangers*, a player is anyone with a business-related objective that collaborates with others who share the same objective. Players in business typically belong to many teams. You can be part of a sales team, a management team, a business development team and a product review team – all in playing the role of National Sales Manager. You hear business people talk all the time about how many hats they wear. Changing hats can definitely be a vexing aspect of working life. You are called into meeting after meeting after meeting. People 'need' you in different ways. One minute you're wearing your green plastic bookkeeper's visor because you're in the middle of a heavy discussion about budgets for the next calendar year. The next minute you're wearing your artist's beret, expected to contribute something visionary to the repositioning of one of your company's brands. A minute after that, your boss wants to know why a key employee is leaving to go to work for a competitor, and all of a sudden you're wearing a top hat to match your tap dancing shoes.

Many Roles, One You

Listen, here's the beauty of the improvisational approach to business: Hat-changing is simply one of those things an improviser does. *You play different roles at work, but always through the truth of who you are!* With the improvisational approach, you don't have to think of yourself as changing gears all the time, or as being pulled in a dozen different directions, which, let's face it, can exhaust anyone. You only have to think of yourself as doing one thing really well: improvisation! Those banes of the traditional workaday world – getting spread too thin, having responsibilities without commensurate authority, being expected to contribute to areas outside your area of expertise – all dissolve within the oasis of improvisation. You never have to be someone you're not. The many roles you inevitably play in the modern workplace are all shaped and informed by who you are as an individual. In improvisation, you are never *not* yourself. When your efforts go toward being yourself, you don't have to worry about being all things to all people.

As the Chairman of Apple Computers, President of Pixar Animation and a member of The Walt Disney Company's board of directors, Steve Jobs is asked to wear many hats. Worn by Steve Jobs, those hats are merely cosmetic, because he knows (and everyone doing business with him knows) they're dealing with Steve Jobs. Business improvisers find success by playing one character – themselves – boldly and entrepreneurially. That's the way it should be no matter how many hats you're asked to wear. *Improvisers focus on being themselves in all situations.*

An old thoroughbred trainer friend of mine, Willie Simpson of New Harmony, Indiana, likes to say, "You can't teach a horse to run any faster than it can run." What at first seems obvious becomes, upon reflection, a pretty insightful statement. A racehorse can be trained to carry a rider, get into and out of a starting gate, allow itself to be paced, run in a crowd of other horses and riders, run in different weather and track conditions – but it can only run to the limits that its natural-born disposition and its equine physiology allow. Nothing you can do with a horse short of drugging it will change its potential. It will run as fast as it can run, but no faster. Likewise, you, as a human being, have skills, education, life experience, mental and physical energy, relationships, imagination, and your human physiology that all go together to determine how much you can accomplish. You can only do so much, right? You can only run as fast as you can run. But here's the big difference between the performance of a racehorse and that of a human. Unlike thoroughbreds, we humans are not always *willing* to run as fast as we can, especially on behalf of our jobs.

We have a lot on our minds. Our emotional interests lie elsewhere, meaning we are beset by 'off-track' diversions. We don't see the point of running at top speed if all we're going to do is go in circles. If we are going to push ourselves to the limits of our potential, we want to know that it's going to get us somewhere, right? If we don't have a carrot dangling in front of us in the form of a juicy stock option package, a year-end bonus or a generous expense account, what's the point? If our good ideas are only going to hit the wall, why keep driving? Consequently, we hold back. We wear masks (that match our hats). We build walls between our business selves and our personal selves. We conserve our passion for the things we really care about. It's as if, one cell at a time, we go about transforming ourselves from Secretariat into Francis the Mule.

Improvisation gives us a way to keep our true selves alive in the workplace and to run as fast as we possibly can in a productive direction. If we are playing well, we contribute to our team's successes and our organization's progress, and we do it by bringing our own skills and talents to the table in full measure. An improviser may wear those different hats, but does it knowing that the hats are only wardrobe, and that wearing a derby with oversized shoes, a cane and a toothbrush moustache does not make one Charlie Chaplin. Beneath the wardrobe and the gloss, we are who we are. The hats we wear do not define us or change our human potential. So forget trying to be all things to all people. Instead, understand yourself as a player who knows how to see, play and, if necessary, change the game.

Again, the true and often-dismaying fact of business life is that a player cannot play any better than a player can play. The good news is that all of us, even the superstars, have a long way to go to play at our best and fulfill our potential as entrepreneurs and as human beings. In this sense, our challenge is a common one, our goals are shared and our business is the same: *Our lives are a continual process of becoming who we are.*

Said the great golfer Ben Hogan when he was 82 years old, "I still learn something new about golf every day of my life." Now understand that Ben Hogan had, in his playing prime, won all the major championships of the golfing world. He had reinvented his swing into a much-imitated thing of perfection. He was acknowledged as the toughest, most intense competitor in the game. And yet, Ben Hogan was still in the process of becoming the player he dreamed of being and continuing to realize *his potential to be Ben Hogan*, until his dying day. That, ladies and gentlemen, is a player.

By using improvisation to help realize our potential for being ourselves in the workplace and bringing the full measure of our talent and passion to every scene we're in, we go a long way toward integrating our personal values, goals and interests into our working lives. That sense of being tugged in too many directions and sapped by having too much asked of us? It derives partly from the sheer time and energy it takes to do what we are expected to do. But the truly enervating situations occur when we are repeatedly asked to compromise, on behalf of jobs and organizations, who we are as human beings. Nothing in the workplace deflates a person's sails more quickly than having their values subverted by the environment. If, for example, you have always prided yourself on your loyalty to your team (and have been rewarded by standout performances) and you are asked by a superior to terminate several members of that team in a move to meet a division budget, you're not going to be very happy about that. You are going to question the support of your management and the wisdom of the people setting the budgets. If you do the hatchet job and go ahead with the layoffs, you will feel as if you're betraying your team, yourself and your ideals. If you renege, you risk being seen as a loose cannon, disloyal to your organization and its business goals. This is a dilemma that, sooner or later, most managers must confront. It's a situation with no easy answers. The agreement you've made with your team is to support them come hell or high water, while the compact you make with your company calls for you to contribute to its bottom line.

Improvisational skills will not make this age-old dilemma go away, but they will help you make choices that are consistent with your values. In the example cited here, you value loyalty to your staff. It's an important part of your identity as a person and as a professional. These people are like family to you. In the scene I have described, you, as an improviser, are going to remain loyal and supportive of your team. Your loyalty could manifest itself in the staunchest possible terms, like making a strong business case why it's important for your team to remain together and refusing to lay them off, even if it could cost you your own job; it could mean that you work aggressively with HR and an outside agency to get the laid-off people placed in other jobs ASAP; or that you fight for more generous severance packages than management initially had been willing to grant. It could mean that you sit down and have a heart-to-heart talk with each of the laid-off employees, and offer them advice based on your own knowledge and experience. In any case, you remain true to yourself, and do not get 'yanked' into becoming someone you're not because of the expectations the company places on you. You are not a hatchet man, a turncoat, a company dog, a backstabber, a double-crosser, or any of the darker sobriquets you could be labeled with if you let the game play you.

The game doesn't play the player, the player plays the game. In the scene above, you stay true to yourself. You are a player playing a role – a responsible manager – that everyone in business, including those you're asked to terminate, understands. Improvisation provides you with a way to play the role while remaining fully committed to the values you hold dear, a way to work effectively in business as a strong and authentic human being.

Scene: In 1950, with the entertainment business still coming out of the global economic doldrums caused by World War II, the banking and investment community laid siege to Walt Disney Studios for the woeful performance of its stock, whose price had been flat for years. Walt Disney's brother, Roy, who managed the financial affairs of the company, could not keep the Wall Street wolves at bay. The institutional investors who held large blocks of Disney stock and the banks to which the studio owed large sums of money were howling for blood, and the blood they wanted was Walt's. They saw him as the problem, a visionary leader whose vision was no longer profitable. It was time, they decreed, for Walt to step offstage and be replaced by a professional manager who heeded the bottom line and the company's responsibilities to its investors. The big investors planned a *coup d'isney* that was to take place at the company's annual stockholders' meeting, held in the main theater on the Disney Studios' Burbank, California, lot. The theater's 390 seats were filled and many more attendees crowded the aisles. Members of the financial press, invited by the big investors, were there too, anticipating the spectacle of the business lynching of a once-mighty but soon-to-be-humbled American icon.

When the meeting began, Walt Disney was not in attendance. Roy apologized, and the tense proceedings got underway. Roy faced tough questioning from the big investors who, in sober dollars-and-cents terms, indicated the need for a change in management. And then Walt arrived, wearing the stylish casual attire he preferred for regular workdays. Nodding politely to a number of people in the audience, including those bent on replacing him, he walked to the podium at the front of the theater, pulled a letter from his jacket pocket and began reading it aloud. Addressed to Walt, the letter was from a couple in Kansas, a husband and wife who owned 20 shares of Disney stock. It expressed their pride in owning the stock, because it made them feel as if they supported, in some small way, the company's mission. It urged Walt to keep up the good work and thanked him for bringing so much happiness into the world.

"*That*," Walt said to the audience, folding up the letter and putting it back in his jacket pocket, "is 'the shareholder' in the Disney company. Now if you'll excuse me, I have work to do."

Without another word, Walt strode energetically from the theater and any enthusiasm for an institutional takeover of his company evaporated in his wake. When viewed as improvisation, this scene shows how a great player plays. Faced with one of the biggest financial crises in his company's history, Walt stepped onstage and stayed deeply committed to who he was: a hard-working producer of happiness, a champion of families and the common man, a believer in the future. The role he played was the founder of a troubled company under fire from the financial community. How he played it was as his authentic self. And because he was so strong and dramatic about who he was and what he stood for, the carping of the big investors suddenly seemed petty by comparison. Of course, history proved Walt's vision far from lost. The 20 shares of Disney common stock owned by the couple in Kansas, had they kept it in the family, would be worth $137,308 today.

What Good Players Do
By defining yourself as a player, you inject all sorts of positive energy into your business life. Let me enumerate a few of the ways:

A good player can play with any team, and any team is happy to have a good player join it. Here's what happens to a team when a good player joins their scene. There's a fresh burst of energy in the room and a readiness for action, because good players take the stage enthusiastically. You feel rewarded by their presence, because you know that simply by strongly being themselves they're likely to contribute something to the scene that you could not. You feel supported, because good players are in the business of taking the situation given to them and spinning it in a positive, productive direction. You feel secure, because good players are reliable – the game you've agreed to is the game you're playing; there is no other. And you feel more confident than ever about the implications of your scene, because good players play on multiple levels. Your scene gains nuance, meaning and stature because of their participation.

Scene: I used to play in a very competitive pick-up basketball game every Saturday morning at Beeman Park in North Hollywood, California. Five-on-five, full-court. Lots of male ego. Lots of woofing back and forth between the many Type-A's who showed up to blow off steam and emotion they'd pent up during the week. One morning, I had the next game and went about recruiting players for my team. A middle-aged black man in nondescript grey sweats looked like he had a pretty decent shot and was in reasonable shape, so I asked him to be on my team. We introduced ourselves. His name was Norman.

Norman and I picked up three other players and we won the next game. There seemed to be nothing exceptional about any of the players on our team. These Beeman Park games featured quite a few flashy street ballers and former college players. Our team had no one like that. As a *team*, though, we played great. Everybody passed the ball, found the open player, set screens and took care of the fundamentals. After we'd won our third straight game, I'd come to realize that this Norman dude was the key to the way we were playing. He was a total team player, scored hardly any points, but every move he made set up a teammate to do something good. Before playing our fourth straight game (an almost unheard-of streak at Beeman), Norman and I were in line for the water fountain, and I said to him, "So Norman, you're a pretty good player."

"Thanks, man."

"You play in college?"

"Yeah, I played some in college."

"I figured. Where at?"

"St. Francis College. Little school up in Pennsylvania."

"Ahh, right. Cool." I'd never heard of the place, but I didn't want to hurt Norman's feelings by saying so. After Norman got his drink, I turned to the person next to me, who was also on our team, and declared, "Norman played in college."

The guy looked at me like he was an astronaut and I'd just told him that things are weightless in space. "Norman played in the *NBA*," he said.

"Really?"

"That's *Norm Van Lier*," the guy said.

Oh. Norman, it turned out, was 'Stormin' Norman' Van Lier, who played for twelve years with the Chicago Bulls, and who I'd seen play on TV dozens of times when I lived in Chicago! Oh yeah. *That* Norman.

In our next game, I paid very close attention to how Norman Van Lier played. It became clear that everything our team did on the court flowed through him. When a player on our team was open, he passed them the ball. If someone needed help on defense, he got there for him. When someone made a mistake, he picked up his own game to compensate. Stormin' Norman played for his team. It would have been easy for him, even in middle age, to dominate the game, but his joy came from seeing his team succeed. And that's how it is with improvisers. Their success is entirely team-oriented. That's why good players can play with anyone, and why a 12-year NBA veteran enjoyed playing with a bunch of weekend warriors in North Hollywood. Team play is one of the joys of the game.

Another important implication of becoming a player is that for the player, *work is a performance.* It's a show with no script, begun by suggestions from your audience. Just as in an improv theater, your work has an audience (your stakeholders, your competitors, your customers), scenes that build and play off one another, and a cast of characters who enter and exit throughout the performance. It lets us approach the tasks at hand in a new, more interesting light. A good player makes informed and rewarding choices, choices that generate the information an organization needs to operate successfully in the Networked World.

There are many outstanding improv teachers at the I.O. West Theater in Los Angeles. One of the best is Jason Pardo, who performs with the brilliant improv troupe, King Ten. Jason, with advice gleaned from author and improv director Mick Napier, of Chicago's Annoyance Theater, gives each new class a handout entitled *Tips to Being a Kickass Student and Powerful Performer*. Here they are:

1. *Be someone who is always on time.*
2. *Be someone who says yes.*
3. *Be someone who listens more than they talk.*
4. *If you must talk, be someone who knows what they're talking about.*
5. *Fuck your fear. Be someone who makes strong choices.*
6. *Be someone who isn't tired or hot or scared. Be vital and engaging.*
7. *Be someone who will try anything. See if it works.*
8. *Be someone who isn't an asshole, even if you are. We're in this together.*
9. *Be courteous off stage. If you interrupt, apologize.*
10. *Be honest. There's no substitute.*

Yeah, be someone like that. It will be a pleasure playing with you.

ENVIRONMENT

OUR FIRST *ENVIRONMENT* IS THE WOMB. It is, for the time of our gestation, our ecosystem. The sustenance we need to survive and thrive surrounds us. It is a place filled with tactile experiences, sound, movement and emotion. We feed from it, learn from it and never stop growing. With our mothers as our partners, it's a nine-month scene that gets edited at birth to begin a new scene called 'Babyhood' that will include many more scene partners and will present us with a more challenging environment than the one we leave behind.

As we grow up, we participate in a steady, lifelong series of scenes that move us farther and farther away from the natural world and into the machined and programmed terrain of adulthood. Today, we live and work inside computers, cars, airplanes, headsets and climate-controlled offices. Those offices are inside buildings that require a security pass so that others know who we are. Beginning with the Industrial Age and continuing today, the machine and the organizations that reflect it are our 'working womb'. Controlled environments come with the territory. The lighting, décor, location of our building and what's in the vending machines have all been decided for us, all in the name of placing as few impediments as possible between ourselves and our assigned activities. These controlled environments don't nurture our activities. Instead, they were constructed to 'not get in the way'. It's like having no environment at all. Our offices are often more tomb-like than womb-like.

During the Industrial Age, we distanced ourselves from the natural world with such speed and force that the momentum carrying us away from it continues to this day. The bread we eat (made from wheat grown, ground and baked by people we don't know) and the bottled water we drink (from who knows where, purified who knows how) are just two examples of how the means of production and the consumer grow further and further apart. And our increasing alienation from the natural world also distances people from one another.

Environment, when it comes to business, does not just refer to ecology, but also to the economic milieu in which business gets conducted. Like the weather, this environment is largely out of our control, consisting as it does of the confluence of behaviors of governments, industry leaders, regulatory agencies, our competitors, technological innovators, disruptive geopolitical factors and the whims of our customers. And as with the weather, when we cannot escape this sometimes-stormy milieu by staying out of it, the best we can do is prepare for it and adapt to it as a matter of course.

I had the good fortune to grow up on a small family farm in Indiana, where the workplace bound up ecology and the economic milieu. This 'ecosystem' supported and nurtured the people who lived and worked within it. We did not control our environment, but we wrestled with it and adjusted to it constantly. A tornado took away my grandparents' barn. Our bottom-land flooded every other spring, and how fast the water receded would determine if we could plant a crop on that land or not, a crop that might mean the difference between a good year or a bad one. Fifteen minutes of hail could wipe out a year's worth of corn. We ate the fish from our own lake and the vegetables from our own garden, and we slaughtered steers that we had raised from the time they were calves, many of whom we knew by name. We tended to the well-being of everyone and everything around us because we knew that, somehow, their well-being was directly tied to our own economic health.

Today, most of us (myself included) work in business environments that are far, far from the family farm. But one of the best bits of news emerging from the Networked World is that we seem to be regaining our awareness of the importance of environment and are moving strongly to reestablish our connections with it. We want to know what's in our food and where it's made. And if we do not exactly live and work in the natural world, we (and our customers) want to be aware of what kind of footprint our work leaves on it. Increasingly, the stakeholders in companies express their desire to have the company directors make responsible moves in this regard. They understand that for a brand to remain an engine of wealth for future generations, it will have to operate in a different environment. Anyone with an investment in the future wants that environment to be a healthy, nurturing one. Some of the most influential brands of the last two decades, such as Wal-Mart and Microsoft, along with a generation of smaller companies have implemented sweeping policy changes and made demands on their suppliers and business partners to become friendlier towards the environment.

All this emphasis on the environment is good news for those who practice improvisation in business. As we emerge from the shadow of the Industrial Age, business improvisers in the Networked World will lead the way in creating new environments – from the Earth's climate to the office cubicle – that will prove the friendliest and most nurturing for the players in an organization. This will not necessarily herald a return to the natural world (I'm not moving back to the farm) but an acknowledgement of it and connections afforded by networked communication that promise to change the very nature of work itself.

Environment, in terms of improv theater, is the stage space within which you work. Allegorically speaking, it is your group's womb, with everything in it you need to make a great scene. If the scene centers on two characters working on a car together, the car, the space and everything in it comprise the environment of the scene. It is a world of sound, movement and emotion. The performers' harmony with their environment enables them to perform with complete conviction, and allows the audience to experience their scene undistracted by questions or inconsistencies.

Those who stage the most compelling business performances in the Networked World will create environments that enable employees to perform with complete conviction, allowing the audience to experience their scenes undistracted by questions or inconsistencies. Sound familiar?

The business environment consists of every possible setting with which members of the organization interact. It invites certain kinds of behaviors and is also affected by the behaviors of its inhabitants. Your business environment is your organization's family farm. This means the *environment should nurture the players*, and by that I do not just mean free lunches, but all the resources available for people to work well together and produce good results. Does your environment tell your brand's story? Is it stimulating visually? Is the lighting good and energy efficient? Is there a place for employees to get involved in physical activity or a quiet place for a five-minute break? What does it sound like? Are the tools you use of good quality, reliable and safe? Ideally, players should feel good about being in the environment, connected to it and know that they had a hand in creating it.

Your audience will understand you better based on the environment in which you conduct business. Environment can bring confidence to investors, attract customers and invite media scrutiny – the good kind, as well as the all-too-familiar exposé. In the Networked World, the world is watching. Bloggers are blogging. Customers are getting savvier. If your business environment pleases the audience, chances are your brand will, too.

There are three kinds of environments with which improvisational organizations and individuals concern themselves: *global, team* and *scenic*.

Global Environment

The global environment refers to the business climate in which you operate. Are you a big player whose every move makes waves in the market? Do you work in a heavily regulated industry? What's the competition like and what's your relationship with them – cutthroat or peaceful coexistence? Do you contribute to the environment or wage war with it? This aspect of the environment, while it's the one over which typical employees have the least influence, can profoundly affect the audience's perception of a brand. Customers are beginning to wise up to the social responsibilities that businesses (and they themselves as employees of those businesses) have toward the Earth and its resources. It's why organizations like the Building Materials Reuse Association have a solid foothold in the U.S. construction market; why Adaptive Path, a leading-edge information architecture group, has had a paperless office since its inception; why the entertainment agency CAA prints on both sides of copy paper; why Wal-Mart hands out three-inch thick binders to all its vendors documenting new, more environmentally friendly standards for manufacturing and packaging, and say to them, "If you want us to sell your stuff, you must comply."

The debate will rage on about whether or not a corporation can actually have any kind of social conscience, but I look at it this way: Regardless of what combinations of market forces, guilt and enlightenment induce businesses to address the environment, it's better for them to do it than to preserve the status quo. In business, as in life, if you do not act, you will most definitely get acted upon. Addressing the global environment, whether we are talking about greening campaigns or tariffs on imports, has the benefit of providing a forward-looking, proactive focus to an organization and its employees. You are making something happen.

Organizational Environment

This aspect of environment refers to the 'vibe' of an organization – its overall physical presentation. What kind of setting greets you in the lobby of a company's offices? Four years' of magazines and a coffee pot with yesterday's coffee in it, or a very cool fish tank? Do you hear music or see video, and if so, what? Is there a wall displaying the company's products? Are people coming and going boisterously or is the place quiet with people speaking in near-whispers? What sense do you get of the company's personality, its people, its story? All those questions are addressed in the organizational environment.

A family farm's organizational environment is pretty easy to see while driving past. Are the fences well-kept? Are the animals healthy? Is the barnyard junky or organized? What hobbies does the family have? Is there a fishing boat or a basketball hoop? Are there flowers and shade trees? A picnic table? Are the old things well-preserved or gone to rust? A company's organizational environment might not be so easily observed while driving past, but it is no less a factor on performance and no less an indicator of the behaviors of its tenants.

Scenic Environment

Scenic environments are the settings for the day-to-day conduct of business by the organization's employees. Scenic environments can but do not necessarily correspond to organizational environments.

When you conduct a meeting on your factory's shop floor, that's organizational environment; it's also scenic, because it's the setting for your scene. Conduct that same meeting at a Cracker Barrel restaurant and, unless you work for Cracker Barrel, it's *not* an organizational environment; but it *is* scenic.

Scenic environments are most affected by employee behaviors and are most akin to the kinds of environments created on the stage for improv theater performances.

Players in business have a choice about the environment in which they conduct their scenes. A skilled improviser looks at environments as carefully as a painter looks at light and color, then creates settings for scenes that will be conducive to achieving the objective. A scene conducted while walking through a park will have an entirely different feeling and, most likely, outcome, than the same scene conducted in a windowless office. There's a reason Wal-Mart's buyers meet all vendors in featureless cubicles. The intention is to grind you on price and everyone knows it. There are no adornments to the scene, no pictures or tchotchkes to hint that a buyer is a softy with a family, a dog and kids in Little League. It's all about the numbers and, from the minute you sit down, you know the focus will be nowhere else.

The environment for scenes set in the Google offices, on the other hand, is lively, chaotic and rambunctious. You'll hear music and laughter in the halls. New furniture, not yet assembled, might be stacked in a corner of a conference room next to recently obsolete computer equipment. Out the large window, you'll see people playing volleyball on the quad, while others ride community bikes across campus for their next meeting. The behaviors of the company are on display in its environment. The energy you get from it is infectious. You are immersed in your scene before a word about business gets spoken.

III. PARTICIPATION

I shall participate, I shall contribute,

and in so doing, I shall be the gainer.

— *Walter Annenberg*

AGREEMENT

IF THERE IS ONE PRINCIPLE OF IMPROVISATION that has the potential to change not only the way business gets conducted, but to change lives, it is this one. Agree! Agree to listen. Agree to play along. Agree to be open to ideas, even those that sound crazy at first. Agree to disagree. In improv theater, you fundamentally agree to accept the realities of your scene partners. In so doing, you build together a new reality, synthesized from two or more points of view that can, in fact, be in direct opposition to one another. This process of agreeing is known as saying 'Yes and' or 'Yes-anding'.

Agreement is the comet to which the improvisational business model is hitched. It enables work to progress apace with the speed of change, and for that work to build in depth and intensity. It liberates ideas and encourages innovation. It gives you a sense of working in a collaborative, team-based environment where you are welcome to express yourself without worrying about the political climate, or whether something will 'fly' with your coworkers or superiors. Whatever you do will fly. That's *The Agreement Principle*. We agree to help one another's thoughts take wing. And best of all, we purge the workplace of negativity and infuse our efforts with positive energy for the betterment of the team and the organization

`"Bad idea."

`"Can't be done."

`"Won't work."

"It's my way or the highway."

"That's not the way we do things around here."

"The last person who tried something like that is no longer with the company."

"Personally I love it, but the boss is going to hate it."

Who hasn't heard these responses to one of their ideas? All the above statements indicate that whatever follows is probably going to be a monumental pain. They are red lights in the traffic of ideas. They will likely lead to conflict, frustration, or just plain lack of joy at performing a job you want to excel in and feel good about.

Negativity is borne of ego and insecurity. It is the default position for individuals who want to control the dialogue by using their hierarchical power to exercise authority. It is the safe haven for people who are too insecure to seek clarity or knowledge. 'Going negative' is the easiest choice for people who are afraid to face their fears. The fear of being wrong. The fear of looking foolish. The fear of losing status or maybe even their jobs. The fear of working without a script. All because they don't know how to improvise.

Agreement, by contrast, opposes negativity by establishing a positive environment for collaboration. By expressing agreement, you open your mind to the possibilities presented by your relationship with other people. Players in a brainstorming meeting who 'yes-and' are immediately thrust into the experience of solving a problem together. Furthermore, the group gives itself many avenues for making progress, and of being open to what the godmother of modern improv, Viola Spolin, called "the spontaneous explosion." A new idea comes alive when you 'yes-and' my idea, I 'yes-and' yours, and we suddenly arrive at what neither of us could have created on our own: an idea that is uniquely *ours*.

"Agreement means allowing the work environment to say okay, we are being true to ourselves, which is about overcoming our fear, and by getting everyone to agree to that we all win together. The risk isn't in trying something that doesn't work. The risk is in not trying," says Roger Fishman of Zizo.

To fully grasp this principle, you must make an important distinction between agreeing to collaborate in the game being played and being a 'yes-person' who blindly agrees with everything. Agreement doesn't mean taking it in the shorts on a deal or giving up your responsibility for making sound critical judgments. Agreement does not mean rubber-stamping. It is not unquestioning, dogmatic acceptance. Notice that the expression used to define The Agreement Principle is not *yes*. It is *yes-and*. It is the *anding* that keeps a scene active and improvisational. Saying 'yes' without 'anding' is its own form of negativity. Being a 'yes-person' may gain you a reputation around the water cooler for being positive and upbeat, but it does not make you an improviser. With the 'and', an improviser supports his or her fellow players by acknowledging their contributions and building upon them. The other players, in turn, follow suit, advancing the scene toward its objective. In this way, 'and' becomes the bridge that connects players to one another and the team to its newly-created reality. I call this process 'playing leapfrog'. We keep advancing one another's ideas and supporting one another's actions until we arrive at the objective.

The Agreement Principle means acknowledging the worthiness of every individual in the group, and valuing the performance of the group over that of any of its individual members. It means that leadership consists of being an outstanding supporter of the team. I'm following you and you're following me and we are following her and she is following him and they are following us and we are all following *it*. The 'it' is the game being played by the group in the solving of a problem. 'It' is the leader. 'It' generates the positivity that binds us, transforms us, and takes us out of our egos, to become one as a group. 'It' is what makes possible the spontaneous explosion that brings something to life that did not exist before.

"You have to envision a different and better tomorrow, and then you have to do everything you can – you have to be relentlessly passionate in pursuit of that vision," says Fishman. "And you have to exceed standards. Whatever the status quo, whatever the benchmarks are in any industry, are irrelevant. Because that's not the way you're going to win, creatively or executionally. You have to envision and feel something different, and then just charge to that. And if you don't believe in it, you shouldn't do it."

An Amish barn-raising is an apotheosis of The Agreement Principle. When an Amish family needs a new barn, they set the environment and initiate the scene by laying the barn's foundation and acquiring the lumber and raw materials to build it. Everyone in the local Amish community joins them onstage and constructs, or 'raises' the new barn. The agreement within this group is to play a game called 'Build a Barn in a Day'. By agreeing to the game, the players commit to their roles and behaviors within that game. They enter strongly, with tools, food and complementary sets of skills. Some are elders who have done this many times before. Their role is to watch over the game and guide it, resolve any disputes, and bring status and history to the experience. Their presence makes this an important event in the community and connects the community to its past. Skilled carpenters supervise the design and construction. They honor the event with their talent. Younger men, in their physical prime, handle the heavy lifting, hammering and roofing. Women make the event a celebration with food and drink and conversation. Children imitate the work being played by the grown-ups and in so doing, honor the game, too.

There could be conflicts within the group. Since when did everyone in a community, even an Amish community, see eye-to-eye about everything? Some of the elders do not approve of the cars driven by the younger folks, or cotton to their style of dress. Some of the new generation have electricity in their homes and send their children to public schools. Perhaps these conflicts have brought deep schisms to certain families. *But they agree on what they are here to do today.* 'It' is the most important thing. 'It' brings them together and lets them set aside their differences. Any conflict subsides within the larger agreement.

LISTENING

THE SKILLS REQUIRED FOR IMPROVISATION are bound up with the art of listening like trees are bound to the soil. Everything begins with listening. Just as the roots of a tree tap into the earth's sustenance so that the tree can grow, listening sustains a scene and enables it to realize its objective. If you're not listening, your scene will never get off the ground. If you *quit* listening, your scene will wither, die, and get chopped up for kindling. And it will happen a lot faster to a scene than it happens to a tree. As renowned management consultant Margaret J. Wheatley writes in her article *Listening as Healing*: "Listening moves us closer, it helps us become more whole, more healthy, more holy. Not listening creates fragmentation, and fragmentation is the root of all suffering."

I once spoke with Wayne Allwine, for many years the head of Disney's Sound Effects department, and the official voice of Mickey Mouse, about the art of listening. "Outside the studio, what do you listen to?" I asked him.

"Everything," he said. "When I'm in a supermarket or an airport, there a hundred sounds that most people don't notice. To me, those are treasure troves." That just about explained it all. Allwine listened everywhere, all the time. Of course, listening for sound effects you might use in a cartoon someday is one thing; listening in a business scene is something else altogether. But forget for a second that Allwine is talking about discovering sound effects. Think of him, instead, like this: He is a businessperson whose livelihood depends on his openness to what's new and unexpected in his field. And so are you.

Listen To…

Listen to the world. Listening to the world helps you make choices that are informed, knowledgeable and current. Players who listen well to the world do it by experiencing the world. They have an appetite for life – for learning, travel and the arts. They appreciate great beauty and great passion. They are open to other cultures, and to thoughts and opinions that are different from their own. They are empathetic, and know what it feels like to walk a mile in someone else's shoes. They pay attention to the macro-economics that affect their work at the micro level. Improvisation, like business itself, is the art of creating unexpected and rewarding connections. The more you experience of the world, the more unexpected and rewarding those connections are going to be.

Listen to your audience. In longform improvisation (and what is a business if not a show with ambitions of a nice long run?), the audience gives a suggestion to the group; from this suggestion, themes are conjured and scenes based on those themes are enacted. Likewise in the improvisational business, you begin by listening to your audience. The suggestions you get – in the form of market research and other types of feedback ranging from casual conversations with your clients to observations of societal trends – become the basis for building your market and your brand.

In business, just as in the theater, the audience tells you how you're doing. You're in the game to please them, and theirs are the voices that matter most. In improv theater, they vote with their laughter, their applause, their attendance – or with silence, groans, squirming, or worse, their absence. In business, the audience speaks with its pocketbook. If they're buying your stuff, you're the one laughing; if they're not buying, you're the one squirming.

Listen to your scene partners. A scene can have quite a few failings and still be a passable scene; listening cannot be one of those failings. For any encounter between two or more individuals to be productive, listening is essential. Many people who think they're listening are only listening to themselves and the audience. Listening to your fellow players – truly hearing what they're saying – is a sign of respect. It is the basis for finding the agreement that allows the scene to grow and morph into something remarkable. And when you are in a scene with a business adversary, it is especially important to hear what they're communicating.

Listen to your coach. When you're in a scene, you're often too busy living it to observe it with a critical eye. In fact, being critical of a scene while it's happening will limit its potential. Criticism, however, is necessary for evolution and growth. This is why improvisers need coaches. In a business scenario, good coaches are typically coworkers who have an innate understanding of *GameChangers* techniques and can lend perspective and offer constructive observations.

So, now that you know *to whom* you should be listening, *what* exactly are you listening for? To repeat Wayne Allwine's advice… everything. Everything is potential material for your success. All your education, every conversation you have, every periodical you read becomes a resource you can bring to your working life. The more you've heard, the more you'll have to say.

Levels of Communication

When it comes to scenes themselves, be aware that there are *three levels of communication* to every human interaction. A good listener hears what's happening on all three levels. A good scene works on those same three levels.

The first level is *cosmetic communication.* This is the dialogue in the scene, i.e. literally the words that come out of people's mouths. It is the least meaningful aspect of communication, but it is no less necessary because of that. Conversational dialogue graces difficult subjects with the aura of civility and adds color and nuance to subjects that are too broad or subtle otherwise. Technical dialogue enters detailed information into a scene, and allows players to work at the level of complexity demanded by the subject matter. Dialogue, however, describes the surface of things, not their essence. Dialogue is to emotion what makeup is to your face. It can be used as easily to conceal the truth as to reveal it.

There have been many attempts over the years by entertainment producers to own and exploit scripts of performances by improv theater troupes. These producers invariably discover that the scripts are relatively worthless. The words, in and of themselves, do not convey their meaning. Emotions convey meaning, and the emotional notes of an improvised performance cannot easily be transcribed to a script.

Emotional communication is the most profound and meaningful level on which human beings interact. Emotions convey most of what constitutes our reality – the forces that have shaped and continue to shape our world. Emotions depict what we want, what we intend, what motivates us. Our emotions govern our actions, and our actions, as the saying goes, speak louder than our words. Good listeners tap into emotional communication (just as good public speakers connect strongly on this level). They do it by listening with more than just their ears. Emotions get communicated with all the senses, and that's how good listening happens – with all the senses. In improvisational theater, we talk a lot about the emotional subtext of a scene. We describe it as being 'what the scene is really about'.

Scene: Two characters step onstage, with one of them playing a (male) Casino Boss, and the other plays a (female) High Roller, the *dialogue* between the two may never stray from the need for high roller to get a credit line extended. That scene, however, will not be about the credit line. The players in the scene know it, the coach knows it and the audience knows it, too. It will be about the relationship between the Casino Boss and the High Roller, and the emotions that characterize that relationship. Is it a power struggle? A seduction? A friendship gone sour? A family rivalry? An attempt to save face? It could be any of these, or any combination thereof. The point is this: If my scene partner and I are playing this scene, the emotional communication is the level on which we focus. This is the aspect that the coach will critique. And, most importantly, it is the communication that will either please or displease the audience. Their satisfaction has nothing to do with whether or not the High Roller gets the credit line extended. The dialogue about the credit line is the surface. Emotions lurk at depth. So use your sonar. You'll be surprised at how much you can hear.

Improvisers in business should likewise focus on listening to and acting upon their scene partners' emotions. Any good salesperson knows that, to be successful, the job cannot be about selling products, but rather about fulfilling the customers' needs. Beyond food, clothing and shelter, these needs are emotional. A skilled salesperson hears emotional cues. Do customers project confidence? Uncertainty? How are they dressed? How do they walk and stand? What gets them to smile? What do they react to? The dialogue between a salesperson and a customer may never stray from the negotiation, but what the customer communicates and what the salesperson hears will be pure emotion.

Scene: Imagine a business scene parallel to the casino scene described above. Replace the Casino Boss with a Vice-President. Replace the High Roller with a Director of Sales. The Director of Sales approaches the V.P. with a request to attend a pricey industry conference on the other side of the continent. They negotiate. Just as in the casino scene, the meaningful communication, what the scene is 're-ally about', will not be conveyed in the dialogue but in the emotional subtext. Depending on the emotions at play, the scene could resolve itself in a myriad of ways:

If the V.P. feels *threatened* by the aggressive request from an up-and-comer, he or she may deny it.

If the Director feels *passionate* about the need to represent their brand at the conference, the V.P. may applaud that passion and grant the request.

If the V.P. and Director have a mentor/protégé relationship, their *camaraderie* will likely result in a pro-forma sign-off.

If the Director feels *dissatisfied* in his or her current position, the request may be the final test over whether to stay with the company or begin looking for a new job.

We carry our emotions into our scenes like we bring baggage when we travel. The baggage can be an impediment to our progress or it can be what makes the journey possible. Either way it's important to listen to and deal with the emotions that are in play in our scenes. If they get in the way, listening helps us work around them; if they have the potential to move the scene forward, listening helps us realize that potential.

Meta-communication is the way a scene represents the issues, ideas and concerns that exist on a societal or universal level, such as a global trend, widely held belief or aspect of the human condition. A scene does not have to communicate on this level, but the most effective scenes do.

In improv theater, a scene involving a mother and daughter

with boundary issues may represent the societal trend of children who move back home after graduating from college. A scene that includes a vote-hungry mayor may serve as a send-up of what people believe to be true about politicians in general – e.g. 'always campaigning for something'.

In business, it is important to listen and communicate on the meta-level because this is the level at which a brand connects with the larger world. Advertising campaigns, where the amount of factual information than can be conveyed is limited, connect with the audience on this level. Mythic symbols (Budweiser's Clydesdales, Merrill Lynch's bull) and scenes (Apple's Cool 'Mac' vs. Microsoft's Nerdy 'PC') are shorthand meta-connections to their respective audiences.

When Dave Neeleman, CEO of JetBlue, represented his brand to the world by publicly apologizing for a spate of delayed and cancelled flights in 2007, the apology resonated in the media because it communicated strongly on cosmetic, emotional and meta levels. Neeleman's actions came about because he and JetBlue listened to their audience. If they had not listened and responded immediately, the negative impact suffered by the brand would have been much greater. Listening on all three levels of communication will ensure that you're in sync with each other, with your market and with your time in history.

MOVEMENT

THE FIRST TIME I EVER LAID EYES on Jeffrey Katzenberg, co-founder and CEO of DreamWorks, he was running up the stairs of the Disney Animation Building two steps at a time. Only months before, in September of 1984, Michael Eisner had taken over as CEO of Disney with Katzenberg as his legendary chief lieutenant in charge of motion picture development and production. Until Katzenberg ran past me that day, I'd never seen a Disney executive take the stairs in the Animation building two at a time. You could characterize the prior Disney administration as bunch of genial middle managers who'd inherited their jobs, meant well, represented the Disney brand to their utmost, but ultimately didn't have much game. (Unless you count the Crazy Eights cards games that half a dozen of the studio's top management played at lunch every day in the executive commissary. My young Disney cohorts and I would look at one another in astonishment and shake our heads at this. What was next? Pick-up Sticks? Would we walk into the commissary one day and find the suits who ran the store fully engaged in a game of Candyland? Because...)

Katzenberg's kind of energy was just what the Disney Company needed at that time to evolve its brand. Katzenberg said more to me that day about who he was as an executive – his excitement about the future, his intensity and focus – than if he'd stopped me on the stairs and spent five minutes reciting his personal vision statement. The way he moved spoke to my emotions. He wasn't running because he was late. People waited on Katzenberg. He was running up those stairs because he had things to get done. Running the stairs meant something, meant more than anything you could cram into a PowerPoint slide. Katzenberg's energy was infectious. I had the distinct sense, based on that very brief encounter, that Disney itself was on the move. And sure enough, over the next ten years, from 1984 to 1994, the thawing of the frozen Walt Disney Company would be one of the great business success stories of the last half of the twentieth century, with major moves that included: the release of the Disney animated classics like *Snow White and the Seven Dwarfs* on home video; the signature urban comedies like *Three Men and a Baby* and *Down and Out in Beverly Hills*; the acquisitions of ABC and ESPN; the partnership with Pixar; Disney Stores; The Disney Cruise Line; The Disney Channel; Hollywood Records; The Disney-MGM Theme Park in Florida and four other new theme parks around the world. It was a truly golden time for the studio. And Katzenberg running up those stairs in the Animation building was the code – *movement as meaning!* – that predicted what was to come.

The Katzenberg story illustrates how movement can convey meaning independently of spoken language. Talented improvisers say at least as much with how they move as they do with the words coming out of their mouths. They underscore and add meaning to their dialogue by their gestures, their posture and their level of energy. If your words and your movement are incongruous with one another, you will be a producer of confusion rather than clarity. If words and movement are strong and consistent with one another, communication between players goes from being simply effective to being profound. The words we use to define our business objectives combined with the way we move, both physically and emotionally, toward those objectives can yield either weak communication or the powerful elixir of a well-told story. The choice is yours.

Less-skilled improvisers often rely too heavily on verbal communication in their scenes. When words fill the vacuum of your scene, you find yourself not conveying enough or even contradicting yourself with movement, like, say, a fidgety engineer trying to convince an audience of department heads that a new design for a production line is solid. When the physical and the verbal contradict one another, what a player means to communicate will get lost, confused or muddled by these mixed messages. As a result, the audience will be lost.

Movement says a lot on the improv stage and should do the same in business. One of the best improv groups I've ever seen, Beer Shark Mice, works at lightning speed. There is never a millisecond of their time onstage where they do not have their audience's attention. At the same time, they never force it. They take their time and modulate their energy. Jeffrey Katzenberg moves quickly, decisively, but without ever rushing things. Beer Shark Mice, the improv group, and Katzenberg, the businessman, epitomize the great basketball coach John Wooden's bromide, "Be quick, but don't hurry." Katzenberg is extremely concise and efficient in the way he moves. He could be doing the silliest bit of schtick (I once shot a video of him where he went through a full day of meetings at DreamWorks Animation wearing an Intel 'bunny suit') and the guy would still mow through his workday.

Katzenberg is legendary for his three-meeting breakfasts and his 'Gong Show' pitches from his development team. I was once sitting outside Michael Eisner's office waiting for a meeting to begin when Katzenberg and two of his development team blew by. I saw Katzenberg's eyes move three times. First to my face – Zip! – who is this guy? Second to the script on my lap – Zap! – mental note to find out what the script is and why Eisner is meeting about it. Third, eyes ahead again – Zop! – focused on initiating his next scene. Three movements, three flicks of the eyes – Zip!-Zap!-Zop! – underscored Katzenberg's mad efficiency. You can tell how he manages his business by the way he moves. His role as head of a movie studio doesn't vary much from day to day, his buttoned-down character might have a bit of a narrow range, but he plays that role to the absolute hilt, even when he's wearing a bunny suit. It can be a little enervating to be around the man full-time, but most people I know who have worked at Disney or DreamWorks with Katzenberg enjoy the experience. The energy he transmits in every scene he's in courses through the circulatory system of his company like blood pumps through a healthy body. It sets an infectious tempo and his fellow players pick up on it.

All productive improvisation uses movement to communicate. In fact, one way you can distinguish a skilled improviser from a not-so-skilled counterpart is by observing how the good improviser communicates with movement. Most beginning improvisers need work in this area. The natural inclination for a beginner is to rely on their verbal skills at the expense of movement. This short-changes the scene. 'Talky' scenes, with so many possibilities for action unexplored, almost never realize their potential. In beginner-level classes at the I.O. Theater in Los Angeles, and at most improv-teaching theaters, students learn to use movement to reveal character and communicate what a scene is about.

What Movement Conveys…and How

Energy. Energy, in improvisational parlance, is the pitch at which the group carries out and modulates its performance. It is the umbrella term for the level of activity and intensity the audience observes in the group and players in the group feel from one another. *The level and kind of energy emanating from an organization is the cumulative energy of its players.* Energy comes in at least as many varieties as Nike has shoes, from good to bad, and all kinds of energies in between.

Some players, like traders on the Stock Exchange or law enforcement personnel, have occupations that naturally manifest a lot of energy. It comes with the job. These kinds of occupations involve a kind of binary activity – you're either on or off – and are not as useful in depicting the importance of movement as other occupations where the energy a person brings to their work is more a matter of personal style.

Project-based occupations like journalism and construction have a natural flow to the energy it takes to do the work – high at the beginning, leveling off in the middle, peaking near completion. I've seldom been in a working environment where the energy was higher and more focused than the day I got to see the weekly edition of *Newsweek* going to press. 'Putting the book to bed' is the operative phrase in the magazine biz. The energy that comes with putting the book to bed was so infectious that it stayed with the magazine's staffers long after they'd left the company. A friend of mine, John Culhane, still has the habit of setting his writing deadlines for Friday, the day of the week *Newsweek* went to the printer when he was working as a reporter there.

In contrast to the on-off energy of physically intense occupations and the arcing energy of periodic projects, the majority of occupations in the Networked World call for players to show up and be highly productive on a daily basis for the duration of their employment. This allows for a wide range of energy with which work can be performed. To be a good player, you want to put out without burning out. Improvisation is just the skill to help you do it because it keeps your internal engine humming without wasting fuel.

Focus. Before you picked up this book, you already knew the importance of focus. Nobody has to tell you what happens if you have no focus and wander through your workday clueless, like somebody in a TV sitcom where no real work ever gets done. If you have no focus, you first lose your scene partners, next your audience, and then you get fired. Most businesspeople can muster enough focus to show that they are competent professionals. If nothing else, our paychecks, fear of losing our gigs or sheer professional pride will give most of us enough focus to see a job through. What separates successful improviser/entrepreneurs from the pack is the *intensity* of the focus they bring to their scenes. We use phrases like 'laser-like', 'in the zone' and 'on a different level' to describe people who bring an extraordinary degree of focus to their work. One of the ways you can achieve that high level of concentration is through movement. Focused movement speaks to your audience.

Jeffrey Katzenberg, like a lot of good improvisers, doesn't waste motion. When he does move, it is with absolute focus on the objective. Good improvisers develop a vocabulary of movement commensurate with their verbal skills. Not everyone moves in the smooth and relentless way that Katzenberg does. Steve Ballmer, the CEO of Microsoft, moves like a guy playing Dance Dance Revolution for money. Many of you have seen the famous viral video of Ballmer at the 2001 Microsoft employees' conference at which he stomps wildly around the stage to the beat of *Get on Your Feet* by Gloria Estefan. The entire text of the speech he makes goes something like, "Yeah! Yeeeeeow! Yeah! Wowowowowow! Yoww!" Ballmer's movement was designed to create focus for his audience (which gave him a standing ovation), by demonstrating his genuine enthusiasm for the work and the product. The cynic in me says that I'd be enthusiastic too if I made as many millions a year as Ballmer does. The improviser in me knows that the way he behaved on that video is how Ballmer has always behaved, and now he's a billionaire because of it.

The kinetic qualities of the great improvisers are at least as eloquent as anything they could put into words. When I was six years old, I had the great luck to see John F. Kennedy one day when he was campaigning for President. My family's car got stopped by the cops at an intersection in Evansville, Indiana, as then-Senator Kennedy's police-escorted motorcade blew past us to a chorus of screaming sirens. I got a glimpse of Kennedy in the backseat of his convertible Lincoln limo, which had its top down and blue-tinted windows rolled up. Kennedy, tan with perfect hair, sat in the middle of the rear seat wearing black Ray-Ban sunglasses, grey suit, white shirt, black tie. I remember how the sun graced Kennedy as his limo passed in front of our car on its way to Dress Memorial Airport in Evansville. It was genius. Kennedy's ability to move through traffic in presidential style so transfixed me that it spoke clearly, loudly to me, even though I was only six. That man was on a mission, with some serious focus on becoming the next President. For those few seconds, without saying a word, John F. Kennedy spoke to me. And I am still listening to what the man had to say.

Movement does not have to be of the showbiz/billionaire/ political glam variety to bring about focus. Most of us, after all, are victims, not beneficiaries, of motorcades. Even if you don't have thirty cops clearing a path for you through traffic, you can achieve focus with other kinds of movement. The kind of move that brings focus to your scenes can be as simple as making good eye contact in conversation. It can be as ordinary as stepping out from behind your podium during a presentation. It can mean bringing lunch to help your team meet a deadline. It can mean taking two steps at a time up the stairs, or taking a bike to work instead of driving. Focus, you see, does not always have to be about the work you do for money. It can characterize every aspect of your life. Any kind of movement has the potential to create focus.

Emotion. One of the many breakthrough moments I experienced while researching this book came when I attended a lecture by Drs. Antonio and Hanna Damasio at USC's Annenberg School of Communications in November of 2006. The Damasios' work is a wonderful synthesis of human behavior and how culture and biology influence it. In particular, the two scientists focus on emotion as the foundation of all human communication and consequently all human culture.

"There isn't anything you can think of that's not influenced by emotion," say the Damasios. They identify two 'states' of emotion: a *Natural* state, meaning that we are always in a state of spontaneous emotion; and a *Learned* state in which emotion has affected past decisions and is now part of the decision-making process. So, yes, emotion is a great big deal.

Like all living things, we are always moving and, as the Damasios would say, never not in a state of emotion. As you might expect, there is a tight correlation between movement and emotion. Call it the Motion/Emotion Effect: *How we feel is how we move and how we move is how we feel.*

Let's first focus on the first half of the epigram: *How we feel is how we move.* Spontaneous emotions cannot be avoided and, on some level, we cannot do anything about how we feel. Your dog dies, you're not going to be happy about it. Some days are just that way. Other days, one would hope, are better. It is only natural that we bring the hue of our current emotional state with us to the workplace.

Obviously, darker, more negative emotions can be extremely counterproductive to getting work done. You do not want to color your day and the working days of your scene partners with downbeat emotions. You cannot afford and your business cannot tolerate a day dominated by doggy death.

So how do you manage the negative emotions?

It is said that some people manage their emotions by being in control of them. I do not believe this is possible. Emotions can be bottled up, withheld and denied, but they cannot be controlled. If ignored or suppressed, emotions will find an outlet, whether it's through a drinking problem or a gnarly pimple in the middle of your forehead. Most people who are said to be in control of their emotions do not control them and do not try. Instead, they channel negative energy into positive. And most of the time, they do it with movement.

Movement is how a good business improviser can manage the negative emotions. The improviser channels it, directs it and refocuses it through by *physically moving* in a way that's productive. We see this process frequently in people who use exercise to burn off some steam or shed anxiety. A good improviser focuses on the second half of the correlation: *How we move is how we feel.* This is where the alchemy happens, where the leaden negative emotions give way to more buoyant, beneficial ones.

The alchemy of transforming negative emotions to positive ones with movement calls on a technique that gets used often in improv theater. "Get out there and do something!" is the ridiculously simple yet hard-to-perform command our coaches repeatedly give us. And here's the miracle of it. When you do "get out there and do something," your movement, by some kind of improvisational osmosis, guides you to a newfound emotional state. *Emotion arises from movement!* An experienced improviser begins making positive moves when things are darkest. Positive movement doesn't have to be dramatic. Dark moods can be directed toward creative activities with amazing results. Anger can be assuaged by acts of kindness. Insecurity can be directed towards attention to detail.

There was a pretty good TV commercial for an airline running in heavy rotation a few years ago that depicted the Motion/Emotion Effect. It showed the head of a company that was having a rough go of it handing out plane tickets to his company's employees so that they could personally visit all their key customers and suppliers. To help his group escape the doldrums, the manager invoked movement. In essence he was saying the same thing to his employees that an improv coach will tell the group: "Get out there and do something!"

The second kind of emotional state described by the Damiasos, the Learned state, also exhibits ties between movement and behavior. We will most likely not repeat what has hurt us before and will in the future behave in ways that have rewarded us. In this emotional state, our movements, like our emotions, are learned through experience. A Vice-President of Sales almost always walks with his or her chin high, chest out, and has a handshake like a catcher in a trapeze act. The V.P. has learned how to move in a way that radiates positive, 'can-do' vibes to his or her scene partners and audience. Improvisers excel in using movement to depict learned emotions. The reason they excel is simply that they are more aware of movement, and more aware of the connection between movement and emotion. It requires practice. The payoff is a new, heightened level of communication between you, your scene partners and the audience.

Attitude. Attitude is a word with a lot of latitude – a broad, catch-all notion that covers everything from your smile to your persistence in the face of adversity. The word 'attitude' comes up more often in business than just about any other I've heard. It gets used a lot with respect to a person's job worthiness, especially if that person is new in the job market, without a professional track record. Sometimes attitude, manifested as a bundle of telltale indicators of a person's approach to life, is the best predictor of how suited a candidate is to a job, particularly when that job is audience-facing. Attitude can be shorthand for the emotional qualities a company seeks in its employees, and, correspondingly, what customers want in a brand. Most employers will tell you they want people with positive attitudes working for them.

Movement is a major conveyor of attitude. How do you project a positive attitude with movement? Do you slump or stand up straight in your scenes? Do you fidget or are you as solid as Tiger Woods over a four-foot putt? Do you stare at the ground or keep your head up when you walk? Do you move energetically or languidly? Movement helps create your personal identity as a player in business.

Movement is the footprint of a company's attitude as well. Mountain Dew supports action sports. The people who work for the brand are themselves a highly kinetic crowd. Google employees balance prodigious bouts of intellectual work with vigorous physical activity. Great restaurants often feature a wait staff that moves with the grace and elegance of ballet dancers. Time and again, for players, teams and brands alike, the winning attitude is expressed through winning movement.

Movement in Media

The amount of movement you generate within the frames, screens and channels that constitute your 'media stage' can, like physical movement, speak to your audience on multiple levels. For example, when movement on your media stage is extreme, you're probably going to be in the youth market. Animation, one form of media movement, is much more likely to appear in a web site geared to a teen audience than one geared toward the health care business. AstroText, a mobile messaging service offering romance-themed horoscopes for teen and young adult women, has a web site featuring a dog named Kitty jumping into her young mistress Simone's arms, and the signs of the zodiac as anime-style teen girls aligning in the AstroText cosmos. And that's just the landing page.

By contrast, Physicians Health, a health care association geared toward physicians and their practices, has no animation on its web site. Physicians Health wants to convey a different vibe to a different audience from the AstroText crowd. The web site's pages, of minimal file size, load very quickly. Information is easy to access. Complex health care rates are made simple. The movement with Physicians Health media is not on the surface of the screen, as with AstroText, but 'backstage' with well-engineered infrastructure that combines three different ASPs (Application Service Providers) into one interface. That's its own kind of movement – one that projects its own kind of attitude.

Symbolic Movement

Sometimes movement takes the form of a gesture or symbolic act that results in energy, focus, emotion and attitude as its by-products. Example: Changing a brand's logo or the name of a company does not, in and of itself, require a lot of physical movement. Legal paperwork, keystrokes, brushstrokes, sign-offs, and the deed is done. The psychological terrain covered in such a move, on the other hand, can be massive, and the physical movement undertaken because of it can be considerable. A merger or acquisition can result in lives being changed, representing a massive amount of *people* movement. A strong symbolic move suggests that a lot of physical movement will follow.

Symbolic moves that stir the audience to action can be among the most fruitful for business. Marketing and PR departments spend fortunes cooking up moves, from 'Subservient Chickens' to flash mobs, that will resonate on a symbolic level with their audience. The money that changes hands in sponsorship deals buys symbolic movement. Brands make the symbolic gesture of sponsoring LeBron James with the expectation that he will, in turn, stir movement by their audience toward points of purchase for their brand.

The fall of the Berlin Wall was a move that symbolized – and will always symbolize – massive relocations of people and wealth. Mythic moves like this are so powerful that they attract the attention of the entire world. When Neil Armstrong said, "That's one small step for *a* man…" (note that he has historically been misquoted on what he said, we are correcting here), he was speaking of his own physical movement in stepping from the lunar lander to the surface of the moon. And when he said, "…and one giant leap for mankind," he was speaking of symbolic movement. Tell me which step, the actual one or the symbolic one, left the bigger footprint?

Be aware, as a business improviser, of your opportunities to engage in symbolic movement. Most good business people are keenly aware of the importance of these kinds of gestures. And they do not have to be big! A truly big, uber-symbolic move may come to you once in a lifetime, if you're lucky. The human tapestry of working life is made up of the thousands of smaller symbolic gestures exchanged within an organization every day. A small gift given, a birthday remembered, praise for our scene partners, a funny story shared, favors done and returned – these are the movements that matter most, because they are the ones that are available to us in every single scene of every single working day.

Get Out There and Do Something!

Most of us, as relative neophytes to the world of improvisation in business, are not very aware of how we move, or of the power of movement to convey meaning. Start paying attention to how you move and the postures you exhibit in different business situations, especially how you use your hands and the angle of your neck and spine. Likewise, pay attention to the movement and posture of others in your scenes. What are people saying by the way they move and use their bodies?

If golfers, dancers and construction workers pay attention to how they move, why shouldn't business people? All of us are trying to produce a desired effect. Golfers are looking for power and accuracy, dancers for pose and animation, construction workers for safety and productivity, and business players for efficiency and sense of purpose, to name just a few of the things that movement can bring about.

So how do you do it? You start by doing the opposite of the lazy, sedentary thing. You merge thought with action. You don't just have good ideas, you have ideas that you and your group can act upon.

Thought is not enough. Thought plus motion gets the job done.

Strong players move quickly and decisively with their minds, and their bodies convey that same quickness and decisiveness. When you walk down a hallway with some bounce in your step on your way to a meeting, you become a person who's got a lot going on. You become magnetic. Your scene partners feed off your energy and, as a group, you move with confidence. One of the reasons director Frank Capra's (*It's a Wonderful Life*) films seem so vibrant is that he'd take care to tell every background extra in a crowd scene their own story about where they were going and what was on their minds. By giving them a sense of purpose, Capra energized their movements which, in turn, communicated to the audience. Movement is the only language a background extra has and Capra was fluent in it. Likewise, the television series *ER* did a beautiful job of giving every single player in every single scene something to do. When you walk into a company's offices and people are moving with that same sense of purpose, the excitement is palpable.

To your audience, movement is one of the most appealing aspects of performance. Sports and other kinds of spectator events aside, think about the times you've enjoyed watching someone do their job. Here are some work moves I can remember enjoying: The adroitness of a Southwest Airlines flight attendant coolly pouring drinks on a turbulent plane flight. My classmate Randy Wagner's dad, Bob, a carpenter, driving nails flush into wood with three easy swings of his hammer. My friend, Glenn Kaino whipping out his PDA like a gunslinger to enter my new contact info when we ran into each other one day in a supermarket. The way Disney animators, back in the paper era, could flip drawings to preview how the scene would look animated at 24 frames per second. The way my friend, the new media entrepreneur Kevin Wall, paces the office when he talks on the phone. The way my father attacked the ground with a post hole digger. When people go about their business in an animated way, it's interesting to watch. Near the end of his career, the NBA Hall-of-Famer, Bill Russell, grew weary of basketball. Every play seemed like déjà vu to him. "We are grown men playing a child's game," Russell observed. "What I'd like to watch is a really good business executive at work. That would be fascinating to me."

One of my all time favorite sites for watching people work is the trading floor at the Chicago Commodities Exchange. You talk about being quick but not getting ahead of yourself, those people have it down. They are all about being in the moment. And it's no coincidence that trades have to be both verbal and visual. The energy it generates on the floor conveys the beating heart of commerce. Movement adds meaning to the thought expressed verbally. It's inspiring, really. "Faith in Industry" is how my friend, the sculptor Clark Ashton of Atlanta, describes the movement that comes with work, and the tonic it can be for whatever ails us.

Google has done an amazing job of building a company culture that involves a lot of energetic movement. Their campus in San Jose has buildings that are spread quite far apart. Community scooters and bicycles make the trek to the outer buildings easy and fun. There's almost always a volleyball game happening on the campus commons.

As you take stock of how you and your fellow players move, ask yourself this: How is my spine? The line of your spine projects all kinds of meaning about what you're up to. If you have the 'hunchies' and walk around like a question mark, chances are something is weighing you down. If your spine is straight like an exclamation point, you're alert, assertive. And if you never bend that straight spine and walk around the office all day like you've got a stick up your ass, people could see you as intractable, unyielding. So pay attention.

The point here is not necessarily to choreograph the way you move or to suggest that you consciously move in different ways depending on the scene you're in. The point is to be observant and aware of physical movement as an important attribute for you and the company you keep. Observing movement in yourself and others will clue you in to how you're perceived, and what people on your team are feeling.

Questions to ask yourself: Am I moving quickly? Am I deliberate? Nervous? Confident? How's my posture? My spine? What kind of handshake do I have? How do I use my hands? Do I nod reflexively, or am I truly listening and agreeing?

The way I move as an individual tells my teammates and the audience a lot about what's going on with me: Can you tell I got whipsawed by the big boss in the meeting just before this one? Is my impatience with a presentation given away by the tapping of my pen? Does my body language say how little respect I have for you? Do I jump out of my chair when I have an idea I want to share? Do I create clarity in the mind of my audience by using my hands to make a description more visual?

The way we move as a group says volumes about our teamwork: Are we excited? Engaged actively or passively? Does our body language say we're ready to support one another? Are we slugs or fleet birds who ride the wind and feed on slugs?

Most of us do not have the luxury of physical activity being built into our work. Lots of us sit at computers all day long. When we're not at our computers, we're in meetings. When we're not in meetings, we're checking our bids on eBay, playing online poker, working on personal websites, or scanning CraigsList for our next jobs. That is a *lot* of sitting around. I've got one word of advice for all of us: Move! Move every chance we get, because the workplace affords us fewer and fewer chances. So get un-cooped when you can. Ride scooters in the hallway. Play racquetball at lunch. Put some pace in your stride. Enter and exit meetings briskly. Don't dawdle. Be decisive and quick. It really does have a magnetic effect. Your group will want to go where you're going and your audience will be keenly interested and engaged in where you're going to take them.

GIFTS

PROSPERITY BEGINS WITH GENEROSITY, so the saying goes.

Gifts, in the parlance of improvisation, are what we give our scenes and scene partners to nurture their development. A scene's fate often swings on how well its players give and take gifts. Gifts also help us get the most out of our working lives and be the strongest versions of who we are.

Gifts are moves that support your scene and the players in it. Gifts are to improvisational business what assists are in the game of basketball – you're setting up a teammate with an easy scoring opportunity and, in turn, increasing your team's likelihood of success. Gifts come in the form of the actions, gestures and information that make others look good and, in so doing, make you look good, especially to your fellow players. They clarify the scene for the audience and help create focus around the objective. In the notes and discussion following a performance, improvisers and their coaches never fail to point out and praise gifts that were given during the show. The act of improvisation is the act of always looking for opportunities to give gifts.

Gifts make a scene meaningful. Giving gifts connects us with our fellow players, creates focus, and brings physical and emotional energy to our scenes. It informs our performances and makes them mean something to us and the audience. One of the most important things I've learned through my own improvisation training is that the more gifts you give, the better you are as an improviser, because it means you're seeing the scene for its full potential. "That was a great gift you gave out there!" is the highest compliment an improviser can receive after a show. If you want your scenes to be meaningful, play the game with everything you've got and give gifts.

Most of the concepts described in this book require translation between a technique as practiced in improv theater, and how those techniques can be applied to our business scenes. Not so with gifts. In business and in theater, gifts serve the same purpose and get executed in both arenas the same way, by *celebrating* something or someone. We all have an intuitive sense of what makes a good gift. There's an element of surprise to a gift and, at the same time, appropriateness. They mark a person or occasion as unique and memorable.

Types of Gifts

Gifts can come in an unlimited number of varieties. Here are some common gifts given in business scenes:

Sometimes it's *a key piece of information* that unlocks a scene and lets it fly. Intelligence on a competitor's upcoming price change is a gift that buys your team some valuable time. An introduction of a buyer to a seller is a gift that can result in a sale. Even a grievance can be a gift that leads to improved working conditions. These are just three kinds of information among many given by the improvisational businessperson. By adding information to a scene, you add to its potential for achieving the objective.

It could be that your gift is *conferring status on another player.* In an improv theater scene, this might consist of making a big fuss over someone, to the point where it gets funny. If, for example, a player portraying a Mom makes a gigantic fuss over a Daughter getting ready for her first date, that player has given the scene and her partner a great gift. We know what that scene is going to be about and look forward to the interplay between the two characters. Making a fuss over someone in a business situation can likewise be good for your scene. We are in a business pitch and I introduce you not only by job title but also as an expert in your field. I have elevated you in the client's eyes and paved the way for the credibility of whatever comes next. When, during a project review, you credit a fellow employee with important contributions to the project, you're giving the gift of status conferred. It may not pay off in that particular scene, but eventually it will. *The full value of a gift is not always realized in the scene in which it is given.*

A gift might be *the start of a pattern* (or in the case of improv comedy, a running gag) that gets called back throughout a performance. The interesting thing about this kind of gift is that you actually *start* a pattern by *following* someone else's action. You cannot start a pattern by trying to start one. In this sense, patterns embody the spirit of improvisation: They require teamwork. If someone in an improv scene makes the statement, "Beets make me feel romantic," there is no way we can predict or expect that it will become part of a pattern, much less what that pattern will be. It is the *second person* who creates the pattern. If the second person responds with, "Beets were the food of choice for the Pharohs," we have established a pattern – 'things about beets'. If, by comparison, the second person responds with, "Broccoli gets *me* in the mood," we have also built a pattern, but a different one – 'sexy veggies'. Either way, the scene has fuel it did not have before. By contrast, compare both of the second-person responses above to a non-supportive response along the lines of "Looks like it's going to rain today." That's no gift. It doesn't mean the scene is without potential, but at this moment, the potential is not being explored.

Look for opportunities in your business scenes to create unexpected and profitable patterns by building on the actions of your fellow players. If one of your fellow players initiates the practice of writing hand-written notes to customers, you create the pattern by writing your own notes, or by adding your own personal touch to your client communication. If someone sells more product by placing it in mini-malls, you give a gift by getting more product in more mini-malls, or by exploring other small, mom-and-pop channels. Not only will patterns make your work more productive, they will help build your company's culture.

Cultural growth of the organization is a huge benefit of the gifts its people give. One employee playing a guitar at lunch is a diversion. Maybe even a distraction. Two employees playing instruments at lunch could be the start of the office band. It is the second person who gives the gift. You see cultural growth in the form of community programs sponsored by employers. After a weekend building a Habitat for Humanity home, for example, participating employees are likely to show up for work on Monday invigorated by the activity, sharing the camaraderie and the sense of fulfillment that comes with…giving gifts.

A gift can come in the form of strong *support from players in the wings*. In improv theater, this means creating sound effects, making music, adding to the environment or voicing offstage characters. *You do not have to be in the scene to give gifts.* The little kindnesses people extend to one another in the workplace go a long way toward making the scenes where business gets conducted more productive. Bringing food, remembering birthdays, and supporting the company's greening initiatives are the kinds of gifts given by players in the wings. When I worked at The Walt Disney Company, a photo editor in the Marketing department named Keith Wainright had a knack (okay, a *gift*) for wrapping gifts. He could wrap any gift box to make it look like a million bucks. Keith was a good photo editor. What made him an extraordinary employee was the support he showed from the wings. He always had a smile on his face. He brushed his teeth at lunch and after snacks. He had a steady stream of people from around the Studio lot showing up at his office with gifts that he would wrap during lunch. I don't know if he ever did any kind of business deal in his life or ever contributed a dime to the bottom line. But his actions served as a daily reminder to the rest of us that happiness was the name of the Disney game.

When it comes to improvisation – onstage or in business – there is one gift so potent that it can be said to encompass and transcend all others. If you give only one gift, and this is the one, it will be a major addition to everything you do. That gift is this: *Make strong choices!* Don't do anything halfway. Don't be soft or noncommittal. Be definite. Be bold. If you decide to take a client to lunch, make a choice about where to eat that will mean something to the client, and add to the scene that transpires there. When you kick off a new project, make it a big deal. Don't limp to the starting line and hope to pick up speed during the race. Enter strong. Play strong. Stay strong. You make a million choices in the course of a campaign, a career, a life. If they are strong ones, you will have no regrets, and the rewards will be commensurate with what you have invested in what you believe.

THE GROUP MIND

ONE OF MY FAVORITE IMPROVISATION EXERCISES, 'Count to Twenty', calls for a group to stand in a closed circle, with players wrapping their arms around each others' backs – their heads bowed, eyes closed. The players count in turn, with the objective of counting to twenty without anyone saying the same number at the same time. If two or more players voice a number simultaneously, the count begins back at one until the group does the exercise 'cleanly'.

Players are coached to avoid following a predictable pattern in which the same people claim the same numbers each time (i.e. I'll always be the one to say "two" and "eight") but instead to feel the flow between members of the group, and to focus on the objective of getting to twenty without two players speaking simultaneously. Try it with a group of four or more players. Newcomers typically stumble through the exercise, while an experienced group, who know one another well, can usually count to twenty cleanly on the first or second try.

How does the experienced group do it? They do it by connecting and communicating via what we, in improv, call *The Group Mind*. The group's focus on the objective generates a very subtle but tangible web of connectivity. We get a sense of who we are – both individually and in relation to one another. This web of connectedness makes itself present by degrees to the group. The more the group works and rehearses, the stronger the web – until it becomes more than a way to play the game or perform a scene successfully. It becomes the reason for the game or the scene to exist. The web of connectivity envelops the game. Our feelings about the group transform from 'otherness' into 'oneness'. *This is who I am* and *This is who they are* become *This is who we are when we play this game* and then, ultimately and profoundly, *This is who we are*. When the players arrive at an understanding of 'who we are', they can count to twenty on the first or second try with regularity. They produce and experience, in the performance of the exercise, the group mind. Finding this state of oneness will be vital to the group's success in performance mode. The group mind is vital to your team's success as well.

In Count to Twenty, no one player is responsible for a number or a set of numbers. No one has to memorize anything. The structure of the exercise makes it impossible for anyone to be 'the leader'. Get too aggressive with your counting and you're inevitably going speak at the same time as someone else. If you're too timid and wait too long, you'll try to fill a silence at the same time others do. Thoughts of individual glory ("I'll get us through this") quickly disappear as ego sublimates itself to the focus ("Let's get through this together"). When we focus, we move as a group toward the objective with the goal of realizing it together. As we move toward the objective, we transform as a group. And when we reach twenty cleanly, we open our eyes, exhale as one, exchange gratified expressions and smile at our success. We did it together. We are connected. We have tapped into the group mind.

Good business improvisation likewise taps into the group mind. Imagine work taking on the quality of the Count To Twenty game. Imagine a shared focus that bonds us with our coworkers. Burdens like time, money and personal ambition get lifted when the group mind lightens the load.

Imagine all the things that keep us from focusing on the objectives of our business scenes – it's an unlimited number…

You're in a stormy relationship, replaying the fight from the night before…the bank just denied a mortgage application for your dream home…your kid's principal calls, telling you your little angel just beat up some other kid during recess. You're distracted. Disconnected. You may even verbally lash out at your teammates. In short, your issues outside the office keep you from engaging in the group mind. And then, of course, there's the number one impediment to building a cohesive group mind: *ego*.

When players act on ego they compete with one another, and the competition becomes its own focus, drawing energy from the stated purpose of the scene. An ego-driven player tries for all the 'punch lines', which, in business, usually translates into having the most noteworthy contribution or the last word. Managers are, of course, most susceptible to the ego trap, because they have people of lower organizational status reporting to them. Who hasn't encountered an ego-driven manager barking at his or her staff, making it clear to anyone within earshot who's the 'top dog'? The ego-driven manager may even find this technique to be effective in the short run. Eventually, however, it wears out its welcome. Instead of the group sharing the workload, they become encumbered by it. The pressure to perform drags down the quality of the performance. Energy and productivity get sacrificed on the altar of the boss's ego. Decisions get made for the wrong reasons.

The ego-driven manager makes a show of choosing one course of action over another strictly to establish the appearance of dominance over the group. Meanwhile, everybody knows that the manager will probably change his or her mind and the group's focus ten or twelve times before the show is over. In this scenario, the only group mind that forms is one of unanimous resentment directed at the manager.

It's not that we don't need our egos. We do. They give us our spine. Our fortitude. Our self-confidence in the face of setbacks. A healthy ego is an important strand in a successful businessperson's DNA. We are tested by the rejection, subversion and duplicity we inevitably encounter in the working world. Breakthrough ideas typically face a daunting amount of resistance. The last mile of the journey from our dreams to a profitable reality can be a hellish gauntlet of creditors and naysayers, and the only thing that gets us to the other side intact is ego. Yes, ego definitely has its place. But, as important as it is, you can afford to shed it like a boxing robe when you step into the ring of the improvisational workplace. You have scenes to do with your coworkers. Good scenes mean working with the group mind. And the group mind means thinking of yourself as part of a group with a shared objective.

Group Think vs. Group Mind

Art Swerdloff, a great industrial filmmaker and film theorist, used to caution me all the time against 'group think'. Art would fly out of his chair when people in an editing bay would acquiesce to a less-than-artful montage of images. "*Group think!*" he'd thunder, "*We're victims of group think!*" Upon which he'd stir up some kind of argument about the merits of editing the scene one way versus another. For Art, and for many intellectuals, the best way to achieve the objective is through a vigorous Darwinian tussle between different ideas that will ultimately synthesize into one 'surviving' idea or theme.

Two points about this approach to collaboration: One, the 'group think' that set off Art Swerdloff is different from the group mind of improvisation. Art's group think had to do with rubber stamping, phoning it in, going with the tide of opinion – all of which he fiercely resisted. The group mind does not mean any of that. In fact, it means the opposite. The group mind allows for wildly different opinions, characters and contributions to a scene. The connectedness of the group mind has nothing to do with commonality of ideas. By honoring the unique contributions of all its members, the team seeks *singularity as a group*. It looks inward for direction. The improvisational business team becomes a mini-network that allows for no end of diversity and individuality. The group mind honors our uniqueness. Business improvisers understand that the power of the group draws distinctive contributions from its members. Strong and varied participation by everyone in the group results in objectives achieved.

The second and more pertinent issue with the Darwinian collaborative process is that no one in business has the time or energy to engage in a *Survivor*-style clash of ideas in every scene. Swerdloff would sometimes stop an editing session and discuss a single edit for over an hour while touching on subjects such as Muybridge photography, Eisenstein's *The Battleship Potemkin*, the origins of modern montage editing and music videos by C+C Music Factory. This kind of process has its place – but in art, not business scenes. In business, decisions must be made swiftly and efficiently. The naturally collaborative nature of the group mind helps this happen. It acknowledges the contributions of the individual while acceding to the hegemony of the group. And with our egos parked at the door, we can move together lightly and quickly over the terrain of the task at hand. Improvisation calls for individuality without ego. *In the group mind, you do not lose your individuality; you celebrate the individuality of everyone in the group.* What you produce as a group will almost always be more powerful than what you could have done on your own. There's a reason racecar drivers talk about how "we" did in a race. They know it's their team, from the sponsors to people on pit row, that enables them to go fast. What the driver provides is focus; it is the team that wins the race.

Kevin Wall and *Live Earth*

The creator and producer of *Live Earth – Concerts for a Climate in Crisis*, the July, 2007 concerts to raise awareness about environmental issues, Kevin Wall, encourages the group mind within his production team. As with every blockbuster concert event he has produced or distributed – *Live 8*, *Pink Floyd at the Berlin Wall* and *The Three Tenors* – most of Wall's projects are originals. They tend to be unprecedented in terms of their cause, their size, their geography, their talent or some combination of all four. There's no road map, yet time and again, Wall pulls off these massive international events with anywhere from six months to six weeks of lead time, striking out on a brand new trail each time. The only way he can do it is by improvising. And improvising means maintaining his group's focus on the objective, no matter what. "You let people know that we're all in it together," he observes. "It's not about me. It's not about them. It's about us, coming together to produce a concert for a cause. I never let anyone forget why we're doing it. That's what brings us together and what *keeps* us together through all the stuff you have to put up with to pull off one of these massive events."

I asked Wall how he explains the objective to his production team. "The objective is not *what you're doing*," he says. "It's *why you're doing it*. The objective of *Live Earth* was not to produce a global concert. If we'd focused on that, we'd all go nuts before we ever got there. There are too many details. It's overwhelming. There are never enough people, there's never enough time. Money is always tight. If it was about the concert, it wouldn't be worth it. People would get pissed off and leave. The reason it's worth it is because of the cause. We're doing it for an important reason. That's what keeps us together and focused. That's why people stay instead of leaving when they get pissed off. Which they do." Wall smiles at me. I am one of those who got pissed off and stayed.

"With *Live Earth*," he continues, "We were out to kick off a movement that would change the world. How often does anyone have a chance be part of something that changes the world? That's what we talked about, what we focused on. And that's why were able to produce an event of that magnitude. We were united behind the belief that by doing it, we could make a difference."

Engendering Group Mind

Wall's *Live Earth* experience can be instructive for anyone in business. Most of you reading this book will have reasons for working that go far beyond food, shelter and clothing. Your personal motivation, however, isn't enough to engender the group mind. Wanting to put your kids through college will not be sufficient motivation for the rest of your group. What is? Sometimes there's a *shared monetary reward* directly tied to the group's performance – as with key executives in a start-up or end-of-year bonuses for employees based on meeting company goals. This is the baseline incentive for all of business. The shared focus can be our paychecks, simply the fact that we are paid to perform our scenes.

Sometimes, by producing an element of danger which imperils everyone in the group, a *crisis* creates the focus from which the group mind grows. You see this in times of natural disasters, when stories surface of strangers working side-by-side or a community closing ranks around its neediest members. Some managers become quite adept at fomenting 'crisis scenes', thus guaranteeing a group's focus. This can be beneficial in certain circumstances but if it's habitual, it can drag down the long-term performance of the team.

Powerful *brands* frequently provide the focus for groups working collaboratively within an organization. In the early 1980s, when The Walt Disney Company was considered moribund by the rest of the entertainment business and much of its shrinking audience, I often experienced this 'belief in the brand' in group business scenes. Nearly everyone at Disney at the time – especially those who had known and worked with Walt Disney himself – believed in the Disney ethos. Whether it was the art of animation, the challenge of producing entertainment with innovations in technology, or a bed-rock belief in family entertainment, teams at Disney could always find reasons why they stuck it out during the hard times.

When the Walt Disneys of an organization are alive and actively involved in the business, their fearlessness awakens the group mind within their organizations. Ted Turner acted as the brilliant improviser who could conjure up counterintuitive yet practical business ideas that fueled flagship projects like the CNN and TNT cable television networks. "Ted tells really great stories and then we all try very hard to make them come true," was how one employee of Turning Broadcasting described the focus of the company at that time.

While the guiding lights of an organization can offer direction and bring about focus, the accomplishments of a company, its basis for succeeding in the marketplace, usually occur elsewhere, away from the bright lights. Collaborative units are the building blocks of networked organizations. These units can have formal designations – Divisions, Teams, Committees, Departments and Groups – but just as often consist of an informal network cutting across organizational lines. Increasingly, teams are virtual and connect by a variety of channels, while face-to-face meetings diminish in frequency. The effectiveness of these collaborative teams rolls up into the overall effectiveness of the organization. In fact, you could say that *a brand's performance is an aggregation of team performances*. How does your call center team do? What's their record? How does your sales team perform? What's their conversion rate? What does the marketing team hear from your audience (and what are they doing about it)? How have employees who joined the company in an acquisition collaborated with the members of the acquiring team? Is your engineering team on the same page as your production team? All these typical performance-related questions have their answers rooted in collaboration, and nothing sets the stage for collaboration like the group mind.

Ernest Hemingway wrote in *To Have and Have Not*, "A man alone ain't got no bloody fucking chance." While we would like to believe that a man alone *does indeed* stand a chance, the fact of life, and of business, is that a group working together stands a better chance than a man working alone.

Benefits of the Group Mind

Among the many benefits of the group mind:

Job satisfaction. Teamwork is a satisfying thing. It's one thing to feel good about yourself. But when you get to feel good for a group, you're going to feel exponentially more satisfied about what you have achieved. The locker rooms of championship football teams are a lot cheerier than the locker rooms of Wimbledon singles champions. Celebrations by winning companies do more for company morale than a noteworthy achievement by 'one who is in our midst'.

The spotlight, shared. In a collaborative environment, everyone gets a chance to be a star. The team dynamic supports players' individual strengths and helps marginalize their weaknesses.

Longevity. Since improvisation does not depend on any one individual, the group mind ensures a brand's successful performance over the long haul. In this sense, we can describe any strong brand, like Budweiser, Motown, or *Saturday Night Live* as an ongoing improvisation. Its founder and its star performers can come and go. The brand plays on.

The genius of boldness and the boldness of genius. Breakthrough success in business involves breakthrough behavior – doing what hasn't been done before. In an ultra-competitive, politically charged corporate environment, it can be difficult for an individual to break new ground. It's risky if not impossible to soldier a big new idea through the system on your own. Think about the bold moves you've made in your life and why you made them. You never would've jumped off the high dive, relocated for a new job or made your first public speech if you didn't have people encouraging, daring, cajoling or demanding it of you. That last decisive push of energy and conviction often comes from the group. *We make the bold, breakthrough move because the group mind emboldens us to it.* To break new ground, to dare to go where you've never gone before, to throw yourself into the fray, it helps to have people in your corner offering their support.

You know the group mind. In some context, however fleeting, you have experienced it before. Look for it in the workplace. Seek it out. Learn how to open doorways into it by nurturing your team's ability to focus on the objective. It will make you a better team player and your team will be better because of it. And if you're some egomaniacal crisis-making nightmare of a manager, it might even make you a better person.

CHARACTER

SKILLED PERFORMERS IN IMPROV THEATER use their training and talent to play many different characters: cops and robbers, the addle-brained and the erudite, people who are high and mighty in the world and those who are down on their luck. It is the job of the improviser in the theater to portray the full pageant of the human condition and give us, in the audience, the gift of being able to laugh at ourselves.

Skilled business performers, by comparison, play only one *Character*: themselves. A player in business may take on many roles and wear many hats, but the character wearing those hats does not change from role to role. The idea in *GameChangers* is to emphasize the strengths and virtues that make you the person you are, bringing unique value to your organization, and to be that person as strongly as you can, no matter what your role. *Business is a performance in which you play yourself.* This is one of two major differences between character in improv comedy and character in business.

The other amendment to the character code in business as compared to improv comedy is that in business *we want to be the best version of ourselves that we can be.* Almost any improv comedy will be populated with its share of charlatans, ne'er do-wells and human skunks. The very nature of satire calls for the improviser to put bad behaviors on bold display for the audience to laugh at. The foundation of business, by contrast, calls for characters who express the virtuous qualities and reliable behaviors that are the bedrock of commerce. Anyone who's been in business for any length of time knows the huge importance of this. All it takes is one unreliable character to torpedo a small business or a growing brand, and we've all seen the spectacle of rogue managers dragging down entire organizations. This, then, is the aspect of character that must be included in any discussion of the improvisational model – not only do players play themselves, you can count on them to do it.

This chapter examines two aspects of character as they relate to the improvisational business model:

One is *being a character*. We will look at the ways in which players can identify their strengths as individual performers, and accentuate those strengths while at the same time eliminating any weaknesses in their game.

The other is *having character*. These are the qualities that let the other players in our scenes know who we are. What they can rely on about us. What they can support. These are the qualities that form the essential compact of all business transactions – that an agreement between two or more players will be as good as gold.

One is what you bring to work with you; the other is what remains at the end of the day.

Being a Character

In the Imaginary Museum of Business, there is a Hall of Characters. The most popular exhibit in the Hall features larger-than-life characters like Ted Turner, Amelia Earhart, Walt Disney, William Randolph Hearst, Oprah Winfrey and Johnny 'Appleseed' Chapman, whose singular lifestyles became inseparable, in the minds of their audiences, from their success in business.

There is an exhibit dedicated to virtual characters who have been conceptualized by their creators solely for the purpose of serving their brands, characters like the Geico Gecko, the Marlboro Man and Mrs. Butterworth.

The largest exhibit depicts local characters – people overlooked by mainstream media who are every bit as colorful and memorable as those who play on the national and international stages. This exhibit is chockablock with folks who dress up in funny costumes to move their merch, who emcee and perform at local events, donate fields to athletic teams, offer college scholarships and perform other acts of charity and public service.

Great characters are among the treasures we take with us from our lives in business. Working with interesting, positive characters is important because they make the entire process more buoyant. They act as anti-drudgery agents, who keep the workday lively. They have gifts they do not hesitate to share. They are good focal points, good conduits of useful information, good supporters of the team.

'Character' consists of a host of personal traits that communicate to scene partners and audiences who we are. Just as we are all improvisers, we are all characters. Of course, we are not all the naturally attention-getting types who will land in the Hall of Characters someday. In fact, when you consider how highly 'public speaking' typically ranks in surveys of what scares people most, you figure attention-getters must be in the minority. The good news is that you don't have to be a rowdy character to be effective in business. In fact, having too many sociable characters around can be disruptive to a working environment. Everyone gets so busy attending office parties and entering football pools that days can go by without any actual work getting done. Being a strong character does not necessarily mean being the life of the party or in a swinging mood all the time. What it does mean is getting a better understanding of who you are – the personality traits that make you unique as an individual and are beneficial to business – and then shining a brighter light on those traits in your scenes.

Johnny Mercer said in one line of music what business pundits have exhausted the dictionary and emptied corporate training budgets trying to actualize: "Accentuate the positive, eliminate the negative… and don't mess with Mr. In-Between." Well, what are your positives? Are you well-organized? Then be known as that character in your scenes. Strongly claim that part of your identity, and wave it around at work like a flag on Independence Day. Be the one who compiles to-do lists for your group or the one who erases the white board before a meeting begins. Who cares whose job it is or what it says about your status in the organization? If it bothers you to see empty cups on a conference table after a meeting, pick them up. If your scene partners have an ounce of improvisational sense, they'll join you in the activity.

Knowing your character means you don't waste time trying to be someone you're not. In the hierarchical organizations of the Industrial Age, employees conformed to the rigidly defined roles they were expected to play. As you know by now, rigidity in the Networked World means rigor mortis for you and your company. The fluid organizational model demands that people be themselves. Diversity of opinion breeds opportunity by creating more options for how to achieve your objectives. By being yourself, you maximize the range of what you can contribute to the company's performance. Also, it's great for morale if people feel they can act in ways consistent with who they really are. The openness created in your company's culture when its people accentuate the positive aspects of their characters tilts the odds in your favor.

We have all been guilty of trying to get away with a cosmetic, surface treatment of our workplace character, one that ultimately conceals more about our true selves than it reveals. We want people to believe we are the designer labels we wear. We want a gadget to earn us the respect of our coworkers. We take up hobbies because they are the boss's hobbies, not because we feel passionate about them ourselves. We obsess over the trendiest restaurants. We hunger for status instead of achievement, until we become like politicians who change positions with every twitch in the polls, whose every word is designed to pander instead of produce. Instead of what we expect of ourselves, we become what others expect of us – until we are nothing but caricatures of our authentic selves.

By contrast, when we act authentically on what moves us, we communicate clearly who we really are. Our passion for the work we do, for our families, loved ones, hobbies – whatever stirs our emotions – adds personality and spreads *joie de vivre* through the workplace. There is a big difference when you drive a fuel-efficient car because you are genuinely passionate about the environment and when you drive that same model because you want others to *believe* you care. The author, Ray Bradbury, once told me, as he has told countless others, that the secret to having a successful career is to "name your loves, then prove your loves." Naming your loves is the cosmetic part of character. Proving your loves is the genuine part.

Just as in improvisational theater, how effectively characters interact with one another in business scenes determines their appeal to the audience. Note that the focus is not on *character* but upon *interaction*. Many of the characters memorialized in the Imaginary

Museum of Business have legendary, larger-than-life personalities. That gives them their visibility. It gets the audience's attention. What gives them their success (and the audience's loyalty) is their ability to play at a consistent level with other productive, energetic, equally compelling characters. When strong characters get together, scenes take off and money gets made.

As an improviser in business, you do not have to own a repertoire of dozens of characters, as most accomplished improv theater performers do. You can be yourself. You can wear many hats, change status, vary the role you play depending on the scene, and all the while perform with the confidence that comes from knowing that the character you're playing is, at its core, you.

Negative and In-Between Characters

Here's something that is both quite obvious, and worth mentioning again. *Eliminate the negative…and don't mess with Mr. In Between.* Negative or muddled behaviors drag down everyone in a scene. They are not productive. They don't lead anywhere and usually stop a scene dead in its tracks.

Scene: Your team has the objective of opening a new market and one player on the team has only negative things to say about that market. He or she doesn't like the major city in the market. It's depressing. Homes are overpriced and schools test below the national average. The demographic isn't a good match for your product. The competition owns the market. The restaurants suck. The weather's lousy. Traffic is bad. The airport is a nightmare. The hotels get burgled on a regular basis. This litany of negativity will go on until it either infects the entire team or gets edited out of the scene. If this negativity persists, it will be much more difficult for the group to realize the objective. Inevitably, every member of the group will have to deal with it and spend time and energy overcoming or working around it.

Mr. In-Between is perhaps an even more maddening type of unproductive player. At least with the negative personalities, you know where you stand. It is possible to identify and deal with negative characters. You can edit them out of your scenes. Mr. In-Between elevates passive aggressiveness to a religion. He is most comfortable in limbo – neither agreeing with his scene partners nor denying them. He is not in the scene, nor is he out of it. You try to edit him out, but he does not leave the stage. He likes lurking on its fringes with a finger in the air, checking to see which way the wind is blowing and jumping in if he's sure he'll look good doing so. He brings no energy of his own to the scene, but drafts off the energy of others instead. He can be supportive, but only selectively so. With Mr. In-Between, you never know what you're going to get. Sometimes he's there for you, sometimes he's not, and he likes it that way.

Scene: Your team has the objective of cutting ten percent from a project budget. Mr. In-Between manages a department whose expenditures contribute to the overage, but he will not commit to cuttng his numbers. As the deadline for delivering the revised budget draws near, he stalls for time. He offers excuses. He changes his mind. A lot. Finally, because he never delivers the requested cuts from his budget, you, as a supportive teammate, do it for him. He shows his thanks by forwarding the complaints from his department's staff to you, sidestepping responsibility for the cuts. Mr. In-Between is playing one of the roles he plays best – victim.

Think about the negative and in-between characters you have encountered in your business life, how they have impeded your scenes, and how much more productive those scenes would've been if they'd brought a different energy to them. Unproductive character traits fall into types that are familiar to most of the working world. Gossips, backstabbers, pessimists and the just-plain-lazy all belong in this category. But before you begin labeling your fellow employees, consider that no one makes the most productive move all of the time. We are all capable of going negative. The reason Johnny Mercer says to eliminate the negative is because we all have it in us. Once we recognize this, it becomes easier to erase negative behaviors from our performance. Likewise, not messing with Mr. In-Between begins with the understanding that he lurks within all of us. It is the natural urge we all have to wait for others to make the first move before we make a move ourselves. His is the voice that causes us to hesitate, doubt ourselves and play it safe. Scenes muddled by Mr. In- Between don't go anywhere and generally die a slow, agonizing death.

Certain character traits that were, in the Industrial Age, deemed liabilities can be surprisingly productive in the Networked World. Experimentation, disruption, risk-taking and irreverence are behaviors that used to be considered controversial but today can work to your advantage. The ever-changing business environment that characterizes markets and challenges companies in the Networked World requires players with no particular respect for the status quo. People who, in the past, would have been labeled 'loose cannons' are now geese that lay golden eggs.

Not every organization will see or embrace the benefits of renegade characters and the disruption they bring. Being disruptive in business does not mean being insubordinate, nor does it mean being negative. It means looking at the death of one idea as the birth of another. It means looking at different ways of doing things and not accepting what is generally accepted. Disruption does not have to hit like an earthquake, but can be a gentle shiver, a tiny shift in perspective that keeps us alert and on our toes. If you think of disruption as a positive force, you will be in a position to reap its benefits. Improvisation is, among many other things, a method for engaging in and managing disruption, a process in which game-changing skills are highly prized and every new game is a new business opportunity.

Becoming a Better Character

Being a character involves more than giving yourself or someone on your team a nickname. It means listening to what your coach and your scene partners see in your performance, then accentuating the positive, eliminating the negative and not messing with you-know-who. It also means being a good observer of yourself. Who are you in your scenes? How do your scene partners react to you? What motivates you? What are your desires? Your dreams?

The thing that always strikes me about great improvisers, one of the secrets to their effectiveness, is that when you're in a scene with them, you instantly know who they are. They define their characters strongly, clearly, from the very first breath they take and, because of that, their scenes immediately have a huge amount of liveliness and emotional involvement.

Here's a short list of characteristics that will, in most scenarios, give your teammates and the audience a sense of who you are and where you're coming from – your worldview, so to speak.

Tempo. At what pace do you work? Are you quick or deliberate by nature? If you're quick, lend your quickness to your scenes by getting things done, not by showing impatience. How quick you can be without tripping over yourself? If you're too deliberate, you will have to work at moving in tempo with the rest of your group or you'll get left behind.

Emotion. At what emotional tone and pitch do you usually work? Are you easily excitable or cool and clinical? Being seen as 'emotional' in business can be a compliment or a criticism. It is a compliment when your emotions help your team focus on the objective. It's a criticism when they are a distraction.

Appearance. This covers the gamut, from your wardrobe to your posture to the car you drive. There's no excuse for being a slob. Your workspace can be cluttered but make it artful clutter, not trashy. If you wear glasses, keep them clean. Be aware of the angle of your spine, your shoulders, of how you use your hands, and where you direct your eyes when you speak. If you are a large person, do you offset it by showing that you are also nimble? If you're compact, how do you make your presence felt? The founder of Ikea, Ingvar Kamprad, drives a 1993 Volvo station wagon. This part of Kamprad's appearance makes him a character instantly identifiable to the Ikea audience. He's one of them – on a budget and likes well-made things that last.

Humor. The person who laughs at every little thing the boss says is a different character from the character who tells funny stories about themselves, who is a different character from the person who laughs at the expense of others. If you have a gift for making people laugh, use it, but use it wisely, with the knowledge that not all laughter is created equal. Overly loud laughter might mean you're insecure. Nervous laughter means you're nervous. When do you laugh and why? It says a lot about your character.

It is our job as improvisers to make who we are as understood as possible – by our scene partners, the audience, and most importantly, by ourselves. Think of character traits as keys on a piano. We play different chords and melodies until, finally, we arrive at a signature sound – *a unique character.*

Having Character

When business people say character counts, they are talking about this kind of character – the human virtues that underpin every successful business venture. These virtues consist of the bedrock values that make business do-able, virtues without which there would be bedlam. If you want to get right to the heart of the matter, honesty, integrity, commitment, trust and overall decency give us the ability to transact without getting ripped off. Business exists on the premise that the people with whom we do business are reasonable, and that we will get a fair shake from them. Our shorthand for this fundamental faith in our fellow players is known as *having character*.

Given all the posturing, positioning and pontificating that goes on in the workplace, having character might seem like a far reach for some players. But let's not confuse the roles being played with who's playing them. A certain amount of ball-busting and misdirection goes on in business — that's simply how the game is played. Players lose money on some deals. Lawsuits get filed. Accusations and acrimony mar some transactions. It's inevitable. Unavoidable. As the adage goes, "If you're not getting sued by somebody, the business isn't worth protecting."

John Lasseter of Pixar does not want to be in the same room as Jeffrey Katzenberg of DreamWorks. Lasseter is convinced that Katzenberg rushed DreamWorks' film, *Antz*, into production to beat Pixar's *A Bug's Life* into release in 1998. When the stakes are high, so are tensions. Those two may never get along. It does not mean that they don't have character. Both of them are highly respected for their achievements and have the steadfast support of their partners, the financial community and their employees. Players line up for miles in hopes of getting into scenes with them. The point is this: There's blood in the business arena. We can get knocked down and hurt. In the end, it is character that keeps us vital, gets us up on our feet and back in the game.

Character does not exist in a vacuum. Anybody can be a saint in an empty room. Character can only manifest itself in relation to other people. A player's ability to *be* a character will not matter if he or she *has* no character. You can put on a good show for your customer audience, but if you don't treat your teammates with at least a modicum of decency, you're a drag on productivity, a toxic character who can bring down the whole team. A company whose players lack character is built on shaky pilings. There's a strong likelihood that eventually the whole thing will come tumbling down.

In addition to the qualities that put the day-to-day conduct of business on reasonable footing, having character also refers to the personal values of players. As the sum of behaviors by all its employees, a company or brand can be said to have (or lack) character. Job skills can be acquired. What employers cannot teach is character.

When employees have character, they become ambassadors for their brand. This amplifies and reinforces the brand's marketing message and comes with the kind of legitimacy that no amount of advertising dollars can buy. Southwest Airlines' company character reflects the resourcefulness and good nature of its employees, because they cast it that way. In the Networked World, there are so many open channels of communication between your brand and your audience that you cannot fake character. The character of an organization – what it stands for – is best defined by the character of its people.

To be strong, character must be tested. When our personal values sail against the twin tides of public opinion and peer pressure, character emerges. When human values supercede numeric ones, it says something about character. When we face adversity of any kind, how we react describes our character. I know business people who enjoy playing golf with their scene partners because they feel that golf, a game filled with adversity, reveals a lot about a person's character.

Having character does not imply that you are of a certain race, religion or political ilk. Those personal distinctions are labels, not indicators of character. They are as likely to conceal a troublemaker as they are to signify a person of honor. When all is said and done, character is how well you treat other people; not just people who can help you, but people who need your help; not just in business, but in all aspects of your life.

IV. Procedure and Process

You can do anything you decide to do. You can act to change and control your life; and the procedure, the process is its own reward

— *Amelia Earhart*

OPENINGS

IN CLASSIC LONGFORM IMPROV, a show that typically runs 25 to 45 minutes with nothing scripted, *Openings* are used to establish the themes explored and echoed in scenes throughout the show. In most improv theater performances, the group takes a word or phrase from the audience and uses this 'suggestion' as the inspiration for an opening. The suggestion is the spark. The performance catches fire when that spark ignites different themes that resonate with the audience. A big reason they resonate with the audience is that the suggestion *came* from the audience. It was their idea. They have a stake in the game.

In business, openings are important because they give your group a way to connect with the audience and get the audience invested in your brand's performance. One of the major sea changes in the art of marketing over the past ten years has been the degree to which companies listen to their audience. Jim Stengel, Chief Marketing Officer for Procter & Gamble, goes so far to say, "Our brands are what our customers tell us they are." With the advent of the internet, taking suggestions from customers has become its own business discipline. Customer Relationship Management refers to a certain kind of software, and it also refers to the act of maintaining ongoing communications with the customer/audience by listening to its suggestions and acting on them. Some very profitable online brands, including Google and Flickr, do this extremely well. In Google's case, suggestions come in the form of search queries;

in Flickr's, photo uploads. Because the Networked World opens so many channels of communication between customer and brand, most companies find it impossible to act on every suggestion from the audience. This is why openings are important. They take the audience's suggestions and turn them into big and mythic ideas. And what company doesn't want to identify and explore the themes that can make their brands mythic?

Scene: Our group takes the stage. One of us steps forward and says, "Good evening, everyone, we are Mud Hen, and we're going to perform for you tonight, and to get things started, may I please have a word, any word at all, from the audience?" Someone says "tomato." The person who requested the suggestion repeats the word – "tomato" – and steps back into the group, which begins its opening. The opening is usually not a scene, but a kind of overture for the show in which themes are developed and 'teased' for the audience. There are many techniques for performing openings, three of which are described in this chapter. Any of these techniques can be used to elicit themes from "tomato." In a typical opening, the group will develop three, possibly four, themes. No more. For example, Health, Romance and Ethics in Science could be themes that emerge from the suggestion "tomato." (See the *Suggestions From the Audience* chapter for more on this subject.)

In the business world, there are many situations that can be considered openings. A business opening can be a morning staff meeting, a speech by a manager to his or her team, the dissemination of an important research report, a business lunch, an initial brainstorming meeting, or any other scenario where you set the stage and establish themes for events to come.

Scene: A morning production meeting at BoxTop Cereals. The meeting is chaired by Don Dunphy, the Senior V.P. of Dry Cereal Manufacturing. The suggestion for the day is "quality control." It seems that a customer discovered a dead mouse in a box of Tastee Bran and there's hell to pay with BoxTop's legal department. The conversation works its way around the room, as the group tries to figure out how a dead mouse might have gotten into the Tastee Bran. They reach a consensus that it didn't happen at BoxTop, that it's probably a hoax by someone hoping to settle quickly before the media get hold of the story. The themes that emerge from this opening might be Integrity, Documentation and Loyalty. For the rest of the day, or for as long as the audience (company lawyers, media, complaining customer) is engaged, the group will involve itself in scenes that develop these themes. Based on the aforementioned themes, we expect this group to strongly defend the integrity of BoxTop's manufacturing process and its products to the BoxTop lawyers. They will document their position for the lawyers with a massive data dump of BoxTop's Quality Assurance process and ten years worth of QA audits in manufacturing. By going to bat for his team, Don Dunphy injects the theme of Loyalty into this scene. It will be up to the lawyers to carry these themes into subsequent scenes.

It's easy to imagine a business opening where the same suggestion by Don Dunphy – "quality control" – results in a completely different set of themes. Let's say it turns out that there *is*, in fact, a mouse issue in one of the BoxTop plants, and that Dunphy's department heads think it's entirely possible that a dead mouse *did* get packaged into a box of Tastee Bran. The themes that develop in *this* opening could well be Honesty, Responsibility and PR. Again, the suggestion is not a theme, it's simply a subject that helps spark the ideas from which themes develop.

How themes get developed in openings is one of the hardest concepts for most improvisers to grasp, let alone do well. Even experienced improvisers can have a hard time eliciting themes strong enough to sustain a performance. Sometimes you only come up with one strong thematic idea and a couple of lesser ones. Sometimes you develop three or four ideas and they are all not-so-great on some level. Sometimes you drum up a theme you've already beaten to death in previous shows and you're bored with your scenes before they even begin. By understanding different types of openings and how they turn suggestions into themes, you'll increase your chances of delivering a standout performance.

Types of Openings
To further understand the alchemy of openings, and how they take a word or idea and turn it into themes, it will be helpful to cite three different classic formats for improv openings. Each of them has elements that can be translated into a business context.

As you read the descriptions of these openings, be mindful

of a couple of things: First, a suggestion from the audience in business is going to be much, much more complex than a single word. It can consist of huge amounts of data generated by research or months' of feedback from your sales staff. Second, a business opening can be a much lengthier affair than an opening in improv theater. Your team's performance will probably last a lot longer than the 30 minutes of a typical improv show. Deep deliberation will usually be required to generate the themes for any brand.

Monologue Opening. A Monologue Opening is exactly what it sounds like. One player stands center stage, takes a suggestion from the audience and uses the suggestion as a jumping-off point, delivering a short (two-minute) monologue from which a show's themes emerge. The best monologues are nearly always based on the monologist's real-life experiences. The players waiting in the wings pay careful attention to the subject matter in the monologue. The audience will not necessarily see these themes at that moment; the other players definitely will.

Owen Burke, appearing as the monologist for the Upright Citizens Brigade's legendary *Asssscat* show, got the suggestion "rigor mortis" from the audience and performed a very funny monologue about having a desk job that he hated, one where his leg would frequently go to sleep while he was doing it. The monologue led the group into themes of Bad Relationships, Hypochondria and Career Counseling. The UCB players pounced on those ideas, resulting in a really wonderful, hilarious show.

A variation of this type of opening is called a *Shared Monologue.* Players perform relay-style, picking up the monologue where the previous monologist left off. It has the interesting effect of creating a mosaic of ideas around the same suggestion. (My ideas about rigor mortis are going to be different from yours.)

The technique used by the business monologist is identical to the one used in improv theater. There is no difference in the technique used by Owen Burke for his *Asssscat* monologue and that of Meg Whitman, CEO of eBay, taking a suggestion like "collectibles survey data" to begin a monologue that leads her team into themes for a new sales strategy. The business version of a monologue opening could be a speech or series of shorter speeches by people familiar with your business. It could come from a high-ranking executive or a management team. It could come from a subject matter expert or a motivational speaker. The speech is given. Themes develop. The group explores those themes in scenes they perform together.

Organic Openings. In this opening, the entire team is onstage. A player steps forward and takes a suggestion from the audience. The group then performs collaboratively to establish themes. An organic opening is a combination of verbal and non-verbal communication. This technique calls for a shared stream of consciousness to flow through the group mind. It works because skilled players can express and build upon each other's ideas fluidly and efficiently. It is a great way to get a group in sync at the beginning of a performance. When an organic opening clicks, you cannot tell who is leading the action and who is following. It is all part of one activity – developing themes.

The business equivalent to an organic opening is any kind of meeting where the entire group collaborates to develop themes for its work. This work could include brainstorming, planning sessions, brand ideation and pitch meetings. For these meetings, I always invoke the 'No Bad Idea' rule, which means that no idea is too silly or far-fetched for discussion, as long as it follows organically from a previously expressed idea. Random, unrelated ideas have the effect of subverting an opening, getting it off-track. A very important aspect of this type of opening is that *new ideas must build off the previous thought.* This keeps the group working together in the moment, ensures that ideas will get explored with some depth, and that the opening will not be too superficial, bouncing chaotically from one topic to the next without ever digging into them in a meaningful way. Let's say an organic opening for an improv show begins with the suggestion "vegetables" and the following ensues:

PLAYER 1: I like potatoes

PLAYER 2: I like them because they're famous in Idaho.

PLAYER 3: I like them because they're stupid and I can beat them at poker.

PLAYER 4: I wish I could be famous for being stupid.

PLAYER 5: I like potatoes because they look good in my pants.

It's too late for Player 5 to start talking about potatoes again. We're now talking about stupid things people are famous for. The 'potato ship' has sailed. By the fourth line (of what may end up being a hundred lines) of this opening, we have spotted a theme: Stupid

Fame. The group should plunge into an exploration of that juicy territory. Anyone who's still thinking about a really snappy follow-up to "I like potatoes" is going to get left behind. Better if Player 5 contributes a statement like, "I want to be famous for a crime I didn't commit" or something of that ilk that stays with the flow of the subject matter. A player who doesn't keep up with the flow of an organic opening impedes the team's progress.

An equivalent business opening might go like this:

PLAYER 1: Bonds are volatile right now with Japan delaying
     its commitment to the Fed.

PLAYER 2: Yeah, it's over North Korea.

PLAYER 3: The whole Asian market is on a 'wait and see'.

PLAYER 4: If South Korea sits down with them in Hong
     Kong next week, new ballgame.

PLAYER 5: I like bonds.

An actual organic opening in business will be much longer, but the idea is the same. You can see that in this conversation, Player 5 was late to the table. The theme is not bonds, it's Volatility in the Asian Markets. It is the obligation of the group to exhaust the idea of the moment. Once Player 3 introduces the topic of the Asian markets, it must be addressed. If, in exploring that topic, we find ourselves back on the subject of bonds, fine, as long as we get there organically. Better if Player 5 contributes to the flow with a statement like, "The Japanese are worried about another liquidity crisis, but the Asian bond market operates differently from ten years ago." Exploring ideas in depth leads to potent openings, with rich, multi-faceted themes spinning out of them.

Invocation. This style of opening is a technique that guarantees going deep into a suggestion to get at the most mythic themes possible. It does a beautiful job of syncing up the group mind at the beginning of a performance. There are four beats to an invocation opening:

    It is...

    You are...

    Thou art...

    And *I am...*

The players begin by getting a suggestion from the audience. They then, as a group, perform an invocation. They do it by making statements about the suggestion that begin with each of the four beats. Let's say the suggestion is "money." An invocation opening based on that suggestion might go like this:

"It is green."

"It is made of metal."

"It is current."

"It features portraits of dead people."

"It is more valuable when you don't know who those dead people are."

"It is minted."

"It is coined."

"It is flipped before games to decide who kicks and who receives."

"It is not worth what it used to be."

"It is named dollar and dinero and baht and yen and Euro."

"It is also named bling-bling and ka-ching..."

After the "It is" statements, the group segues into the next beat, which *personalizes* the word. The players' emotions and energy heighten as they invoke these ideas:

"You are the stuff banks are made of."

"You are the reason we're in this mess."

"You are worth fighting for."

"You are what Robin Hood robbed from the rich and gave to the poor..."

"You are the reason Robin Hood's men are Merry."

"And why Maid Marian wants him to marry her."

"You are what I'll have more of when I win the lottery."

"You're what gets me out of bed in the morning."

"You're my new yacht."

Next it's time for the beat where ideas get *dramatic*. Players get very theatrical, with Shakespearean-style histrionics, during this beat:

"Thou art the coin of the realm."

"Thou art what politicians suckle as the calf to the maternal teat."

"Thou art the billionaire's billions."

"Thou art what doth not grow on trees."

"Thou art the pitiful fruit of mine labors."

"Thou art buried in dead men's chests."

"Thou art stashed in mattresses and freezers by crazy people."

"Thou art what I doth not take to mine grave."

Finally, the players *embody* the word, turning it into a full-fledged creation, imbuing it with a range of larger-than-life emotions.

"I am the power to make nations…"

"I am the weight of the world…"

"I am what's in your wallet."

"I am what's on your mind when you can't sleep at night."

"I am your worst nightmare and your dream come true."

"I am the difference between Donald Trump and You."

"I am the difference between You and You…and You"

"I am Donald Trump…"

For the finale, on the very last line, everyone in the group takes a step forward, theatrically raises right hands in unison and proclaims loudly, spiritedly …

"I…AM…MONEY!!!!!"

The "money" invocation described above brought at least half a dozen solid themes to life. Seasoned improvisers will naturally gravitate toward themes that they know from experience will bear fruit. In this opening, for example, Politics, Power and Insecurity are three themes the group could choose to explore. What other themes can you spot? Notice, as I have said before, that suggestions are not themes. *The suggestion is the spark that ignites thematic ideas.* An entire 30-minute improvised show could arise from the suggestion "money" and the word may never come up again, because it's not a theme.

Based on the above example, you may think an invocation is useless in the world of business. On the contrary, an invocation is one of the most powerful techniques in the entrepreneur's repertoire.

Forget about the format and the four beats for a second. You don't have to be so literal. In improv comedy, the invocation is a highly stylized, theatrical opening. *In business, an invocation is any process that helps players personalize and embody themes.* It might be a company outing, employee training, a motivational seminar, or any number of situations where a group is expected to assimilate ideas essential to the conduct of the company's business. Think of it like this: When it comes to business, an invocation is the talk that helps you walk the walk.

Mark "Dill" Driscoll, founder and president of *ignition*, inc., an Atlanta-based experiential marketing company, has his company's teams stage daily invocations when they're on location for a client.

"We want to make a positive difference on behalf of our clients," says Driscoll. "And to do that, we've got to be true to ourselves. We've got to treat people well, and support one another in everything we do. Our invocations are our daily reminder." An interesting aspect of the *ignition,* inc. invocations is that they happen at the end of a working day. (An opening, in business, does not always have to come at the beginning of a performance. New themes can be invoked or existing ones recalled whenever needed.) "We talk about the good things that happened during the day, things we're thankful for," says Driscoll. "We talk about what we're going to do differently or better tomorrow. The most important thing our invocations do is give us a chance to express our respect for the people on our team."

Del Close, the improv legend who taught two generations of genius improvisers at Second City and I.O. theaters in Chicago, once performed an invocation for one of his classes. That invocation became a legend in and of itself. In it, Del Close invoked *Del Close.* His name was the suggestion. Think about it. And then try it yourself. What would you say as your *It is/You are/Thou art/I am* opening if your own name is the suggestion? Be honest. No one has to hear it but you and your pets.

Opening Tips

Now that you're familiar with the concept of openings, here are a couple of tips to help nurture the development of themes for your business scenes.

Don't go broad, go deep. In other words, instead of covering a little ground on a lot of topics, cover a lot of ground on very few topics. Imagine that the group in the first Tastee Bran scene had 'gone broad'. Going broad could mean talking about the ball game last night, the price of gas, the upcoming union negotiations, those General Mills takeover rumors, and this mouse-in-the-Tastee-Bran mess in legal – all as part of the same opening. You can't develop strong themes out of a free-ranging, ultimately random discourse like that. Narrow your areas of exploration and explore them more thoroughly. This is a good advice not only for openings, but for all the improvising you do.

Work from the outside of an idea into it. Note that in the invocation opening, the suggestion first gets *examined from a clinical distance,* with an impersonal third-person pronoun (*"It is…"*). We then *warm up the idea* by welcoming it to second-personhood with "You are…". The idea is now, in our minds, a being. It is a 'you'. Next, we *dignify* our creation with *"Thou art…"*. And then we actually *become the idea* it with "I am…" statements. This approach of working from the outside in is valid for all openings, and a great way to get buy-in from your team for your ideas. Approach your business openings in the same outside-in way.

The Walt Disney Company's employee training program, Disney University, begins its executive training by showing the new hires an introductory film about the company (It is animation…. It is ESPN…It is ABC…etc.). It concludes with those new execs wearing Disney character costumes for a day in one of the company's theme parks ("I am Goofy!"). It is much more rewarding and effective for a group to *become* something, compared to following an assignment to *be* a certain way. The joy of work, the joy of life, is in the becoming. Openings are a great way for any individual, team or company to develop the themes that become their brand.

In most business organizations, it is very important for employees, particularly when facing an audience, to embody the company's brand. Countless hours are spent ensuring that an organization's customer-facing performances are on-message and authentic. Themes like Efficiency (FedEx), Design (Apple), Style (Martha Stewart), Service (JiffyLube), Tastiness (Hostess), Energy (Red Bull), and Happiness (Disney) permeate the cultures and operations of our organizations. The big brands generally do a good job of invoking their themes. Those companies have spent many years and billions of dollars invoking salient themes in every form of media. But you don't have years to do it, and you probably don't have billions of dollars, at least not yet. So what are you going to do? You are going to invoke your themes anyway, because it doesn't cost anything to improvise, and it doesn't take years and billions to start. And you're going to start immediately, since time and opportunities are always in short supply.

SUGGESTIONS FROM THE AUDIENCE

AN INCREASINGLY COMPETITIVE AREA of differentiation between brands is their attentiveness to their customers (thus the abundance of polling, CRM feedback loops, and audience-generated media). Customers call the shots. Customization is the name of the game. This focus on the customer plays perfectly into the improvisational model. Attention to the customer begins with what improvisational theater calls *Suggestions from the Audience*.

In the *commedia del artes* of the Renaissance, when improvisational theater began, small troupes of performers traveled from town to town in Italy and central Europe, giving spontaneous shows on street corners. These troupes used satire as a way of appealing to the locals' sense of humor. Before the show began, these street performers would gather as much information as they could about the town and its people. Who the bigshots were. The name of the constable. The concerns of the citizens. The performance would then arise organically from the conversation with the audience. Because the troupe had been given useful information and invariably had a repertoire of stock characters that figured into the life of every small town, they could customize the performance with satirical scenes that the audiences found hilarious. Sanctimonious officials would get punctured in parody. The concerns of the citizens would get addressed in the themes of the show.

When David Shepherd revived *commedia del artes* with his formation of The Compass Players (a forerunner of Second City) at the

University of Chicago in 1955, he wanted a way for his troupe to recreate the local appeal that had characterized the shows of the Renaissance street performers. Someone suggested taking suggestions from the audience and a staple of modern improv theater was born.

A suggestion is the word(s) or idea(s) given by the audience to an improv group from which the group develops themes for a performance. Suggestions are important to improvisation because *they make the audience an active collaborator in the show.* Watching a group springboard from a suggestion into an exploration of themes inspired by that suggestion is one of the most engaging aspects of an improv performance. It engenders a natural rapport between audience and performers, and gives the crowd a rooting interest in the outcome of the show. ("After all, it's *our* idea – it *must* be good.")

The business improviser also acts on suggestions from the audience. The purpose is the same: *to bring the audience into active collaboration on your brand.* These business-related suggestions are highly complex and come in a multitude of forms via many channels and, if the organization is wired at all, in heavy volume. Business suggestions have more in common with the dialogue between *commedia del artes* performers and townspeople of the Renaissance than they do with the suggestions that typically kick off a modern improv comedy show. Why? Those *commedia del artes* suggestions came from a *community describing itself.* In business, the community describing itself yields the themes upon which improvisational companies build their brands.

Marketing executives like Jim Stengel, the CMO of Procter & Gamble, who understand that brands are, in effect, improvisational performances for the marketplace, spend millions of dollars and much of their division's strategic focus every year 'listening to the community describe itself'. The improvisational marketers call on their brands to reflect what the community says. A multi-billion-dollar company like P & G and a centuries-gone *commedia del artes* group from Italy have this vital fact of life in common: The success of each hinges on how adept they are at developing brand themes and satisfying performances out of suggestions from their audiences.

Who is your audience? The forces that shape your brand emanate primarily from the audience. Customers, non-employee stockholders, competitors, the media – anyone observing the organization from the outside – comprise your brand's *external audience*. Everyone involved in the day-to-day running of the organization whose approvals are needed to move work forward comprise the brand's *internal audience*. This audience's approval does not determine or guarantee success in the marketplace, but success in the marketplace is not possible without it.

Depending on a player's role within the organization, the importance of one audience over another can vary. A CEO has the board of directors to consider as an audience; a shipping manager probably will not. Every employee in an improvisational organization recognizes and respects suggestions from their internal audience. But when all is said and done, what the customers are saying matters most. You can have all the buy-in, respect and support in the world from your other stakeholders, but if you lose your customers, you lose everything.

Suggestions from the Customer

Forms in which suggestions from the customer audience come to business organizations include the following:

Market Research. Ah, good-old-fashioned nuts-and-bolts market research! Polling. Focus groups. In-store interviews. Product sampling campaigns. Online questionnaires. What self-preserving executive would make a move without the numbers to back him or her up? I am personally ambivalent about market research. There has not been a failed product brought to market in the past fifty years, from Beta VCR tapes to the PeaPod online grocery service, that did not have some kind of encouraging market research to justify the investment. I think there is at least as much, if not more bad market research cited in business as there is good.

By 'bad market research' I do not mean that the numbers aren't valid. They usually are. Market research is an extremely sophisticated data-gathering craft and, when used well, can be a huge boon to a company's strategy and tactics in the marketplace. By bad market research I mean researchers who conspire with the players who hire them to interpret the numbers in a politically advantageous light. By bad market research I mean when players 'script' the numbers, reading them in a biased way to support a personal agenda. By bad market research I mean players get so inundated with data that they end up trying to find the common denominator, and end up being commonplace in the marketplace as a result.

An early episode in my professional career forever skewed my opinion of market research toward the skeptical end of the confidence spectrum. The Walt Disney Company, where I was a senior staff publicist at the time, produced a film entitled *Astronaut in Camelot*, a retelling of Mark Twain's *A Connecticut Yankee in King Arthur's Court*.

The research for *Astronaut in Camelot* came back with a recommendation from the researchers that the title of the film needed changing. The new title they were recommending? *The Unidentified Flying Oddball!* No one could believe it – not the managers who commissioned the research, the researchers themselves, nor the younger people in the marketing department who thought everyone involved had lost their minds. But there it was, in the hard data the managers cited. The managers, who did not trust their own creative instincts on such things, decided to roll with the research, to predictably disastrous results at the box office. *The Unidentified Flying Oddball* bombed.

The problem with market research, you see, is not with the data, but with the inconsistencies, insecurities and personal prejudices that bias the evaluation of the research. By contrast, *GameChangers* techniques provide businesspeople with a way of acting on market research intelligently and instinctively, yielding strong themes and actions in support of their brand's performance in the marketplace. *GameChangers* turns the human factor from a weakness into the most powerful part of the research equation.

Customer Relationship Management (CRM). Suggestions from the audience to the organization are not only a prologue to a performance, they flow non-stop via the CRM networks made possible by the internet and mobile devices. In some instances, as with MySpace, eBay, Flickr, Second Life or other social networking platforms, CRM and the product itself are so connected as to be indistinguishable. The community, in describing itself, *becomes* the product! CRM has grown into its own specialty within marketing and, in many companies, is the life's blood of the marketing strategy. The best CRM programs establish a dialogue between the company and the audience. Sales prospects and records, marketing media, customer recommendations and product customization are all abetted by CRM.

Suggestions offered via CRM should be used more as a means of heightening and exploring existing brand themes than as a bellwether of some radically new direction for the brand. In the improvisational model, look at CRM as feedback from the audience. Is that applause you hear? If not, it may be time to edit your current scene and get started on a new one.

One-to-One. The most powerful and meaningful form of communication is person-to-person interaction. We may find our enthusiasms, our fads, and our distractions in one-to-few and one-to-many scenarios, but what lasts in life, and what gets business done, is what we say and do one-to-one. This is why suggestions that come directly from another person are the ones entrepreneurs and business improvisers take most seriously.

In 1998 Dr. Taryn Rose was an orthopedic surgeon practicing in San Francisco. Her patients included quite a few stylish, shoe-loving women who frequently complained to Dr. Rose about and needed treatment for foot pain – pain caused by those stylish shoes. The complaints were so chronic that Rose took them as a business suggestion. From the suggestion of "hurting feet," the entrepreneurial physician arrived at a theme of Comfortable Fashion and began designing shoes that appealed to her audience's sense of style and her doctor's sense of good health. Suffice it to say that Rose no longer practices medicine. Today, she is a well-documented business success story, the founder and CEO of Taryn Rose, Inc., which in 2007 will enjoy retail sales worldwide in excess of $20 million.

As an executive in the health care business, Tamara Sibson, by contrast, heard complaints from *doctors*. The health care plans available to physicians, their families and their practices were laden with limitations on treatments, paperwork and slow reimbursements from insurance companies. Based on a suggestion that could be summarized as the first line of the Hippocratic Oath – "Heal thyself" – Sibson spent seven years developing a new health care plan geared specifically to health care professionals. In creating the marketing plan for her new company, Physicians Health, Sibson and her team took the many hundreds of one-to-one suggestions they received in those seven years and distilled them organically into the themes for the Physicians Health brand: Relationships, Empowerment, Balance. Sibson assesses her company's financial performance like every other

CEO – Sales, ROI, EBITDA. The financials, to Physicians Health, are the measure of how well the brand delivers on its themes, themes directly descended from seven years of suggestions by the audience. Suggestions from the audience are, in fact, so important to Physicians Health that the company has formed what it calls an Exchange, an online forum for physicians where the best suggestions for health care reform will get worked into company's product offering as a matter of course.

"I'm a big observational guy," said P & G's Stengel, in a profile in *Fortune* magazine. Stengel has moved his company's emphasis away from focus groups and into one-to-one sources of suggestions. He encourages his marketers to invest time observing consumers – watching them wash clothes, clean floors and change diapers. A few years ago, they spent four hours a month with consumers. "It's at least triple that now," Stengel said.

As stated above, there are many audiences, external and internal, that affect a product's march toward consumer acceptance. It is important to take suggestions from them all; but the suggestions that develop into themes for a marketing campaign come from the most important audience of them all – your customers. They, and they alone, determine your fate in the marketplace.

INITIATIONS

INITIATIONS ARE THE FIRST SIGNIFICANT ACTIONS taken by the players in a scene. A strong initiation generates the energy and information to set the stage for the rest of the scene, while a weak one leaves players floundering and the audience impatient for the scene's intentions to become apparent.

Skilled improvisers have the ability, in very few words, to instantly engage the audience in what's happening now. A strong initiation opens the minds of players and audience alike. Imagine yourself being able to enter a scene, any scene, and have everyone in the room comprehend your point of view, ready to go along for the ride.

In the presence of a strong initiation, we get hooked in the moment. We have no choice. *What's going to happen here? We want to know!* Our natural human instincts to seek completeness, unity and resolution in a situation take over. Curiosity may kill the cat, but it's how human beings get where they're going and become who they are in the world. A strong initiation will stir the audience's curiosity in the time it takes you to read this sentence.

Scene: You are in a two-company bake-off to win new business from a big client, one whose account will guarantee that you meet your revenue targets for the year. Like a lot of audiences, this customer/audience is skeptical. This is the third time you've pitched them and you're rightfully concerned that they're jaded by now. Your competitor has substantial history and deeper relationships with the client. And on top of all that, you hear that the competitor has been spreading malicious, untrue rumors about your inability to manage this account. Now imagine you're the player who initiates the scene on behalf of your group. And what you do is...spend five minutes describing what the scene will be before the scene actually begins. You walk the audience through your PowerPoint table of contents, reading every single word projected on the screen, as if your audience isn't already reading way ahead of you. You try to set their expectations. In so many words, you promise them that this is going to be the most stupendous...eye-opening...extravaganza...of a business solution... ever to....

If I'm in the audience and I've heard this pitch two times before, I'm not buying your hype. Three minutes in, I sneak a peek at my watch, wondering how long this is going to take. The familiarity of the scene allows my mind to drift. I find myself reading ahead in the handout. I wonder if your competitor's vicious rumors are true. I wonder if I should text someone about being late for my next meeting. I could use a cup of coffee, would it be rude if I go get it now? Damn, I just remembered I need to Google the reviews on that car I test-drove last week. I wonder if I can get away with doing it right here?

A far cry from the focus you want from your audience, right? By spending all that time making promises of what's to come, you vacated the moment and consequently lost the opportunity to seize it. Since you didn't emotionally engage the audience through your first words or actions, you now have go about reeling them back in, a much more difficult proposition. A strong initiation invites your audience to take its first taste of an irresistible dish you're preparing before their very eyes. A strong initiation is an appetite-whetting step toward a new, mouth-watering reality.

There is an old saying in the giving of business presentations: "Tell 'em what they're going to see. Tell 'em what they're seeing. Tell 'em what they saw." Well, you can store that rusty saw in your tool shed and forget about it. Audiences in the Networked World are not the yokels of yesteryear. They don't need to be told what they're seeing. They see. They can process information prodigiously. You're onstage to show them something they haven't been shown before, do something they haven't seen done before. That's the word. *Do*. In the improvisational business model, you do not *tell*. You *do*. Anyone can *talk* a big game. The question your audience wants answered is who can *play* a big game. And the way you tell them that a big game is coming is with a strong initiation. An initiation does not predict, telegraph or narrate. An initiation *does something*. Don't *tell* your audience how you're going to fulfill their business needs. *Fulfill* them!

Scene: You are in the same bake-off as before. Same skeptical client. Same venomous competitor. Again, imagine you're the player who initiates the scene for your group. And what you do is... produce a box of Girl Scout Cookies and inform your audience that Girl Scouts are the secret weapon behind their next campaign. You pass around the cookies while continuing your scene...

This time, as the audience, I'm thinking, Girl Scouts? What are they talking about? We sell garden equipment (or securities or travel or technology)! What does door-to-door baked-goods-hawking by bunch of knobby-kneed pre-teens who aren't even close to our target demo have to do with us? Are you actually going to suggest we hire Girl Scouts? That'd be nuts. I do like these cookies, though. Thin Mints are my favorites but these DoSiDos are a close second. I wonder if anybody will notice if I take two? I wish people loved our product the way I love Girl Scout Cookies. I wish our brand got the emotional response theirs does from their customers. Wait, what do they mean by "secret weapon?"

See the difference? The first initiation describes something to come. The second plunges right into the business of becoming something. The first is passive. The second is active. The first, predictable. The second, surprising. The first, analytical. The second, emotional. The audience for the first has to wait for the scene to begin. The audience for the second gets involved straightaway in the action. In the 'Girl Scout Cookie' initiation, your audience is given a focus – an idea absolutely loaded with questions and possibilities about the scene to come.

But wait just a Samoan second, you say, it's *gimmicky* to give out Girl Scout Cookies to open a business meeting! Here's the thing, though – a strong initiation is *not* a gimmick. It is the foundation upon which you build your scene. If you don't end up building a scene on it, then it's not an initiation at all, because it doesn't lead to anything pertinent. In that case, you'd be right to label it a gimmick. So that you can fully understand the difference, let's continue thinking about the Girl Scout Cookie move...

If you make the Girl Scout Cookie initiation, let's say as a way to establish yourself and your group as 'offbeat and different', and then never mention Girl Scouts Cookies in any relevant way again, you're living in gimmickville. If, on the other hand, the initiation leads to the central conceit (the game) of your presentation, if you use it to explore a theme or themes that are relevant to your audience – let's say in this instance it's the effectiveness of one-to-one marketing – then it's not a gimmick at all. It's the first taste of what will be a full-blown dish by the time you and your group are finished cooking. If your aim is to win the business with a very cool one-to-one marketing campaign, the code for everything inherent in that campaign – how the client's product is sampled and sold, what the customer experience will be, how brand loyalty is maintained, how the product line evolves, how new markets are opened – all of it is embedded in a Girl Scout Cookie.

Initiating Strongly

By definition, an initiation initiates. Many business encounters, like the one described in the first scene above, don't initiate anything. They start soft and can take forever to get up to speed, if they ever do. Remember this about initiations: *They contain the metadata for the rest of your scene.* Encoded in it are the themes, characters and relationships that persist throughout a performance. If the initiation is soft, the scene will be, too. "Everything we are and everything we are to become is contained in initiations," says Jason Pardo of the Los Angeles-based improv group, King Ten. As a teacher, Pardo will sometimes work with a class for an entire three-hour session on nothing but initiations – ten seconds long, then five seconds, 30 seconds, five minutes or until he stops you – they are that important to successful scenes.

The first step in a strong initiation is to make sure you're initiating something, even if you don't know what that something will turn into. It is okay to step onstage and have only the germ of an inspiration for the scene to come. Sometimes it's best that way. The strongest initiations are simple, symbolic and very definite in their tone. Pop! The cork explodes off the champagne bottle. That's the effect of a good initiation.

Want to know the best way to guarantee a good initiation? *Lead with emotion!* This is the second vital trait of a strong initiation. Nothing is more immediately identifiable and interesting to your audience than an emotional point of view.

In improv theater, we play with a wide range of emotions, from suicidal despondency to wild euphoria. The darker, more negative emotions are included in the repertoire of any experienced improviser, but audiences respond best to brighter, more positive emotions – it's true in improv shows, it's true in business, it's true in *life*. Sometimes, business involves the art of delivering bad news. There's nothing you can do to make a missed deadline a positive thing. What are you going to do now? You can approach the situation with positive energy. When you are playing in the moment, positivity is always possible. Positive energy wins over your audience much more easily than negative. Positive, upbeat emotions are the only way to go.

Think about the emotions you're bringing to your scene with the Girl Scout Cookie initiation. You are asking your audience to see the universe from the emotional point of view of an 11-year-old Girl Scout. You are buoyant, friendly, optimistic and giddy with life's possibilities. You have unshakeable confidence in your great product. You are in the business of putting smiles on your customer's faces. An initiation with those upbeat emotions can't help but carry the meeting and make it fly.

The third vital trait of a strong initiation is this: *Get right to it.* Don't beat around the bush. Don't hem and haw, and how-do-you-do, or wait to see what choices other people in the scene are making. Don't stall for time, deliberate or crack jokes. Make a strong choice, open your mouth and trust whatever comes out. In workshops, Pardo coaches his students to say something the second they step into the scene. He doesn't even care what that something is, because the focus is on getting right to it, whatever it is.

The fourth piece of coaching I've found to be invaluable in making good initiations: *Be yourself.* Be who you are from the get-go. When you step onstage, you bring with you every one of your life experiences, all your knowledge, insights and imagination, and most importantly, how you feel to the full range of your emotions. Why would you go to the trouble of trying to be someone else? Be someone you're not requires a lot of effort. Direct that effort into being as good as you can be in your scenes.

Even the strongest initation does not guarantee a good scene. Given the gift of a strong initation, you and the players on your team have to know how to follow up on it with the fundamentals described in this book. Here's the best all-around suggestion I know for turning initiations into good scenes: *Stay committed to the initiation.* Make a strong first move, then go with it, go where it takes you. If you initiate with Girl Scout Cookies (or recent market research, a new direct mailer, a revised timeline for your project), you are hitching your scene's fate to that idea. That's your deal and you're sticking to it. As the DNA code for what you want to communicate to your client/audience, it must persist or you're lost, and so are they. How many times have you been involved in presentations or projects that lose their momentum? Often, it happens because we're too willing to give up on our initiation. So we pander to our audience instead, or get bogged down by questions and sidebars. We are all familiar with the pressure to take that route. *Don't!* Other players with other ideas can enter a scene you've initiated. That's okay. The audience may react in an unexpected way or not at all. Doesn't matter. *Start* strong and *stay* strong. Do not get rattled or thrown by seemingly contradictory or contrary points of view.

As a way to better understand initiations, think back on some of the business meetings you've participated in that have been particularly productive, ended with a strong sense of mission, with everyone energized and focused on the tasks at hand. How were they initiated? What were the emotions at play in these scenes and what initiations put them into play?

Examples of Initiations

Following are some real-world examples of initiations. You will see the traits described above inherent in the strong ones and lacking in the weak ones.

Missing a Certain Something. On the DVD included in Charna Halpern's book, *Art by Committee,* Tina Fey and Amy Poehler (who found fame on television's *Saturday Night Live*) perform a scene together. In it, they sit somewhat formally across from one another in the middle of the stage and Tina says to Amy, in a professionally condescending tone, "I read your manuscript, and it seems to be missing a certain something." Period. That's it – a very simple but immensely effective initiation that contains all the metadata for the scene. It describes who they are and their relationship to one another: editor and writer. It describes Tina's emotional state: mild disappointment tinged with a ray of hope – maybe this manuscript can be saved if the certain missing something gets put in. It suggests an emotion for Amy (hopeful) that she can accept as a gift from Tina, or choose her own emotion. It suggests where they are – these two are not socializing, Tina's character is too business-like for that. They are in Tina's office. All this information gets processed by the audience as Amy absorbs it and responds. The audience is *with* the scene. When Amy says, "Yes, I have slept with *many* famous celebrities," the audience laughs in recognition. The initiation doesn't do all the work, but it is such a great gift from Tina that by the second line in the scene, the audience is fully aware of what the scene is about and emotionally invested in its outcome. Here is a writer who wrote a tell-all without telling all! Will she tell or won't she? Who are the famous celebrities? Will the book get published? If it gets published will Amy herself become a celebrity? The scene between Tina and Amy later morphs into several others that continue themes like Privileged Information, Celebrity Worship, and the Power of Secrets. All of it was embedded in Tina's brilliant, one-line initiation.

Green Party. This legendary initiation happened in 1979, in South Bend, Indiana, in front of an audience of 60,000, just prior to a football game between the Fighting Irish of Notre Dame and the University of Southern California Trojans. The two schools have a storied football rivalry dating back almost a hundred years. Often, the perceived success of their entire football season – with millions of dollars in merchandising, television revenue, alumni contributions, and the clout to lure blue-chip recruits to their programs at stake – hinges on this one big game. Momentum has a way of shifting back and forth in the series, with one school holding sway over the other for a number of years before the pendulum swings the other way. This year promised to be a very close game, and perhaps one of those pendulum-swinging years. Both teams were undefeated and loaded with All-Americans. Joe Montana starred at quarterback for Notre Dame. Charles White carried the load for USC at running back. Notre Dame's coach at the time, Dan Devine, was a thoughtful, soft-spoken man, more in the mold of a college history professor than the intense, aggressive coaching personality Notre Dame fans expected to see leading their players into battle. Yet on that perfect Saturday in October, he produced one of the great psychological masterpieces in the history of college football. The initiation he dreamed up was so strong that the game's outcome was a foregone conclusion before it began.

Here's how it went down: Notre Dame warmed up before the game in its traditional dark blue home jerseys. Two generations of Fighting Irish fans had come of age cheering for the blue-and-gold colors of their team. Generations of USC fans knew those colors, too, as belonging to their greatest rival. After their pre-game warm-ups, both teams returned to their locker rooms for last-minute instructions from their coaches, and to gird themselves mentally for the great battle to come. Just prior to kick-off, USC returned to the field. And then, Notre Dame ran back out the locker room tunnel onto the field and a wave of electricity jolted the stadium into a new level of consciousness. *The Irish had changed into green jerseys!*

It is impossible to describe the huge emotional impact this had on everyone there that day. The excitement and confidence on the Notre Dame side skyrocketed. The wearing of the green contained the metadata for the rest of the scene. The element of surprise. The invincibility of 'Irish wearing green'. A break with tradition that at the same time seemed deeply rooted in mythic lore. USC, meanwhile, appeared suddenly flat, demoralized, beset by unanswerable questions. What does this mean? Why are their fans so excited? It was like they were suddenly facing an opponent for whom they had not prepared. And that's how the game went. USC performed liked they'd been kneecapped by leprechauns. Notre Dame routed them, 42-23.

Over the next fifteen years, Notre Dame teams would try to pull off the green jersey initiation many more times, but the impact was never the same. The spontaneous explosion of a new experience never erupted again the way it did that first time, thanks to the quiet genius of Dan Devine. On that day, on that stage, he changed the game with a legendary move.

The Wow Factor. I was, at the time this happened, head of Creative for a large internet consulting company. We were getting ready to pitch Mazda for its online business, potentially worth millions of dollars. The founder and CEO of our organization, a hard-charging Atlanta media baron named Bert E., directed that we should spare no effort or expense to win this business, explaining that we badly needed a client in the automotive industry to round out our portfolio and boost our stock price. Bert assigned Chuck C., our head of Business Development, to carry the flag for this campaign. "We need a wow factor," Chuck exhorted me. "Something that'll blow their doors off and set us apart from the competition in the first five minutes of our pitch." Hmm. Wow factor, eh? My team brainstormed an initiation. With Chuck's approval, we sent video crews to half a dozen Mazda dealerships around the country and interviewed their sales managers about how they thought the internet could be used to build walk-in traffic, test drives and, ultimately, sales. Then we wrote a three-minute script for Chuck and edited the video interviews to set up an initiation where we had the Mazda dealers conversing with him as if they were live on satellite feeds. Of course, their sound bites fit our scripted pitch like a driving glove. It worked well enough in rehearsal, but it wasn't enough for Chuck. "We're still missing the wow factor," he complained as the day of the pitch drew near. "This is good, but it's not *wow* good."

For the next few frantic days, we ran stuff up Chuck's flagpole to see if he'd salute. None of it was the wow factor he was looking for. And then, at the eleventh hour, more out of desperation than anything, I suggested, "What about skywriting?"

Chuck, whose dad was an ace fighter pilot in the Korean War, snapped to attention and saluted the flag. "Now *that*," he exclaimed, "is a *wow factor!*"

Mazda's slogan at the time was "Get in. Be moved." Our initiation called for a skywriter to etch the words GET IN across the sky outside the conference room. We would begin the pitch in dramatic fashion, by asking the Mazda executives to step to the long conference room window, whereupon we'd yank open the curtains and show them half their brand's mantra filling the sky. As they turned back, our presentation screen would have the words BE MOVED on it. The underlying theme was that our campaign would marry old and new media in a way that would generate more Mazda experiences in the marketplace and direct more potential customers down the 'purchase funnel'.

The day of the Mazda pitch dawned partly cloudy – not exactly ideal for skywriting. We were prepared, though. If the clouds took away our first option, we had a back-up plan. A second airplane towing a banner that said GET IN would circle a couple of miles away from the Mazda building, on stand-by. If the clouds obscured the blue sky, we'd switch to Plan B ten minutes before we began, and have the banner towed past the window at the lowest possible altitude. Sure enough, ten minutes before pitch-time, we got word from our skywriter that the cloud cover was too heavy. Not a problem. We coolly switched to Plan B. The pilot of the banner-towing plane – who had flown several dry runs earlier – got alerted that he was the go-to-player in the new initiation. We coordinated watches…

There were 30 people in the room for the presentation – 15 in our group and 15 Mazda execs in the audience. Precisely 90 seconds into the presentation, Chuck asked the Mazda folks to step to the window and take a look outside. Right on cue, we yanked open the curtains to reveal – *nothing!* No plane. No banner. No wow. Not even a factor. It was the longest minute of our business lives. What had happened? At the door of the conference room, I spotted a production assistant frantically gesturing and mouthing words that I could not understand. I looked down the row of 30 faces profiled along the window – the startled expressions of my colleagues and the puzzled Mazda faces. No one on our team knew what to say or how to go about salvaging the scene. Then it got even worse. The Mazda execs began cracking jokes.

"Is it the concrete truck?" asked one.

"Is it the lady with the baby?" asked another.

Pretty soon, to our horror, all of the Mazda execs were lampooning what they were supposed to be seeing out the window.

"Is it the guy mowing grass?"

"Is it that *bird?*"

"Well, that didn't work," our CEO, Bert, finally drawled in a huff, closing the curtains on the failed initiation. "Let's get on with it."

We segued to our mock satellite interviews with the Mazda dealers which, not surprisingly, had lost their luster in the wake of the banner disaster. And not only that, for the entire time Chuck did those mock interviews, we could hear the banner-towing plane flying back and forth outside, on the other side of the closed curtains…

MMRRRRRRRRRAAAAWWWW…MMRRRRRRRAAAAW-
WWW… as if mocking everything we were saying inside that
conference room. It turned out the pilot had been prevented from
hitting his mark by the sudden appearance of two Air Force fighter
jets directly in his flight path. By the time he could fly ahead, Bert
had pulled the curtains. The pilot tried to make up for the missed cue
by flying back and forth a dozen times, but it was too late. When we
found what had happened, the perfectly legitimate 'Air Force excuse'
held no consolation at all.

It will come as no surprise to anybody reading this that we did
not win the Mazda account. A weak initiation can keep a scene from
ever getting off the ground. The real lesson learned in this story is
that a strong initiation has nothing to do with creating a Wow Factor.
Your first shot cannot be the killer shot. Payoffs for scenes can only
come later on. A faux satellite feed or even a lady with a baby could
have kicked things off just fine.

You Can't Eat That! An initiation for a sales presentation that's
legendary within the Case Foods Division of the Procter & Gamble
company goes like this: A salesman walks into a buyer's office carrying a can of Crisco shortening. The salesman pops the lid off the
can of shortening, pulls a spoon out of his coat pocket and begins
eating Crisco out of the can. The buyer says, "Are you out of your
mind? You can't eat that!" or incredulous words to that effect.

"Exactly," says the salesperson (who's really eating whipped
cream from the Crisco can). "You can't eat Crisco by itself. That's
why you need a double-end-aisle display of Crisco *and* Duncan Hines
cake mix this holiday season."

Night of the Writer. Perhaps in an homage to the classic Robert
Mitchum film, *Night of the Hunter*, Dave Schiff, Co-Creative Director for the powerhouse Miami ad agency, Crispin Porter + Bogusky,
has the words 'NOUN' and 'VERB' tattooed across his knuckles.
After any initiation where those tats are on display – say as he pulls
a presentation out of the vintage 1950s suitcase in which he carries
his work – how can you not take the guy's work seriously? He's committed. He's authentic. He's copywriting. He's Advertising.

Toilet Talk. In 1984, I conducted the first video interview Michael Eisner gave as the newly appointed CEO of The Walt Disney
Company. The interview, he decreed, would take place in his private

conference room. To my uneasy surprise, a dozen executives from the Marketing, Publicity and Corporate Communications departments showed up that day to witness their new boss's first official Disney interview. They sat around the large conference table, at one end of which I'd set up the camera and lighting for the interview. When we were ready, someone notified Eisner, who entered the conference room then promptly excused himself to an adjoining bathroom, where for five minutes he got on a business phone call and talked loudly enough for everyone in the conference room to hear. When he came out of the bathroom, he said, sheepishly, "Sorry about that." Everyone laughed. Ha-ha-ha. A strong initiation? Maybe. Maybe not. On one hand, who wants to spend five minutes at the beginning of a meeting imagining their new CEO on the toilet? On the other hand, this initiation came to characterize the kind of hard-charging, round-the-clock business style for which Eisner and his management team became known over the next 20 years. In that sense, you could say the CEO made an effective initiation. Eisner certainly communicated clearly to his staff that he was a player who does deals anytime, anywhere.

Wells Rappels. Eisner's 'secret weapon', Disney President Frank Wells, made his first appearance to the studio's employees by rappelling down from the rafters of Disney's biggest sound stage on a mountain climbing rope. Wells was an avid mountain climber and adventurer who'd climbed six of the seven highest summits on each continent. His appearance conjured up great energy, surprise, adventure, risk-taking and a sense of playful fun that was very much in keeping with the spirit of Disney entertainment. It was even tied to the company's history and culture. (Years earlier, Disney had released a film called *Third Man on the Mountain*, which in turn became the inspiration for Disneyland's Matternhorn ride.) Very strong.

Back From the Moon. While we're on the subject of The Walt Disney Company, here's one of my all-time favorite initiations, by Walt Disney himself. During the construction of Disneyland in the early 1950s, Walt's 14-year-old daughter, Diane, was 'writing' a *Saturday Evening Post* series about him – later compiled into a book entitled *My Dad Walt Disney*. For the most part, Diane was fronting for a ghostwriter, a reporter and celebrity biographer named Pete Martin. Martin acquired source material for the book by conducting a series of interviews with Walt and family at the Disney home in Holmby Hills, a suburb of Los Angeles. For one interview session, Walt showed up late. He'd been in Anaheim, overseeing the construction of his new theme park. He made himself a drink. Martin switched on his tape recorder. Walt sat down next to Diane and began the interview by exclaiming, "I just got back from the *moon!*" Martin spent the next 15 minutes of the interview trying, with Diane's help, to decode everything embedded in that wonderful initiation. Walt Disney was as good a business improviser as there ever was. With strong support from his brother, Roy, he continually reinvented the Disney company, while always staying completely committed to the themes and ideals upon which it was founded. Walt had great energy and, with eyes and ears open to the world for inspiration, an unwavering confidence in his instincts. When he proclaimed to Martin that he just got back from the moon, it was the essence of the man – his love of technology and invention, his relentless optimism about the future and a childlike sense of joy at experiencing something new. An initiation this strong sets the stage for any scene that follows – a book interview, a Rocket to the Moon or a new direction for a classic brand – to be a richly rewarding experience for the audience.

ENTRANCES, EXITS, ADDITIONS AND EDITS

ENTRANCES AND EXITS SPEAK VOLUMES about your confidence as a player, your commitment to your scenes and the cohesiveness of your team. *Additions* and *Edits* add useful information to scenes or end a scene at the appropriate time. Your audience will read as much into these cues and make as many judgments based on them as anything else you do. No other skills more visibly underscore the difference between a GameChanger and a grunt more than how you enter, exit, add to and edit scenes.

Entrances

In business, an entrance occurs anytime you enter a room, step in front of a group to give a presentation or meet others for the first time. When you enter a scene, the audience will be reading your body language. They will form instantaneous opinions about you and your group based on how you enter. A skilled improviser steps onstage decisively, energetically, without any hesitation or doubt.

Entrances are not a purely physical action. Physical movement is motivated by an emotion or idea the improviser wants to convey. With entrances, as with all other aspects of improv, *entrances are motivated by intention and an emotional point of view.* What are you thinking when you step onstage? How are you feeling? What's your idea for the scene? What is at stake? When you've got something provocative going on upstairs and it motivates your entrance, the audience will pick up on that and will be naturally intrigued by what's going to come next. When you enter strongly, your audience is with you from the get-go.

Timing and *good energy* are also essential to effective entrances. Energetic, well-timed entrances can be made in ways that are consistent with one's personal style. No one should expect a boisterous entrance out of a bookish character. The style of entrance is not the issue. Style is a personal matter. The issue is whether you step into to your scenes when necessary and with appropriate energy.

Let's look at a typical business scene where the entrances are poorly executed:

Scene: You are asked by Patricia, your company's head of sales, to speak to the national sales managers about a product upgrade that you, as a lead software engineer, and your team are developing. Although the upgrade isn't finished, the Marketing and Sales divisions have committed $3 million against the launch date. You feel that engineering, as usual, is the dog getting wagged by the company tail and you're not happy about it.

You decide to send a message to Patricia that you're too busy busting your ass to meet their arbitrary launch date to come to her meeting. Instead of attending, you send Brandon, a wet-behind-the-ears junior engineer, to speak to the sales managers. As a responsible steward of the company's brand, you have your priorities in order, right? Well, you may think so, but as an improviser, you are in the process of initiating a couple of really bad scenes.

Because 'you're busy', you do a poor job of prepping Brandon. He shows up for the meeting late, unprepared and clueless, looking more like someone who wandered into the room by accident than the presumptive main character in the scene. He exudes uneasiness and uncertainty. The sales managers, smelling the fear, pounce hard, attacking poor Brandon with challenging questions for which he has no good answers. Patricia, incensed, adjourns the meeting early and summons you into another meeting with her and your boss, Arch, the head of engineering.

Scene: Uh oh. By now, you know you've done wrong. You enter the scene with Patricia and Arch like a dead man walking. Your guilty entrance provides Patricia with her cue to hang you in front of your boss. Her sales team, she fumes, is now less than enthused about the quality of the new product, all thanks to you, Mr. Righteous.

A scene can fall apart for lots of reasons, but a bad entrance tips the audience early that a scene is going to have problems. By engineering a couple of lame entrances, you have now steered two scenes into the wall and guaranteed that, should anything go wrong with the launch of the new product, you're going to be the scapegoat. Furthermore, you put your boss in an awkward situation with one of his peers and possibly sabotaged the career track of an unsuspecting junior engineer. Congratulations.

Entrances cover a lot of territory. Here are a few more familiar entrances that most people will recognize as not-so-hot for business:

Dude, Where's My Dongle? Some little missing piece of technology, like a dongle or an adapter, hangs up the start of a presentation. We have picture but no sound. Sound but no picture. No picture, no sound, no clue. An executive know-it-all tells you to try pressing Control-Alt-Shift-Escape-F11, to no effect.

"We'll be just a minute, we have to send for an AV person."

"Does anybody want anything to drink while we're waiting?"

"Yeah, a double martini, two onions and your ass on a skewer, as soon as this meeting is over."

When the props for your presentation are not tested and ready, you're setting yourself up for a bad entrance. Your scene will suffer because of it, and so will you, as a performer.

Casualty Friday. It's one thing to work in a relaxed atmosphere – most people perform better, long-term, in that kind of environment. When the casual approach turns into sloppiness, however, the quality of work begins to suffer. Symptoms of Casualty Friday include: lethargic, low-energy behaviors at the beginnings of scenes; people straggling in after meetings have begun; people entering while talking on the phone; and blurring of the line between professionalism and sociability. Meetings that don't start on time, capricious cancellations and extended deadlines are also signs of over-casualness. Waiting in the wings and not entering when you're expected to or entering distractedly undercut the potential of any performance. These 'poor entrances' cost companies a lot of money in the form of hours wasted.

Star Turn. People who consider themselves 'star performers' will indicate their status by keeping the rest of the team waiting before finally making a dramatic entrance, at which point the scene can commence. This attention-getting stunt is, generally speaking, a poor entrance. I was once in a meeting where we were all waiting on the top-ranking executive to arrive. The exec had just called to say he was stuck in traffic but not to start the meeting without him. Right after that phone call, a straggler showed up for the meeting, and when we informed her that the top exec was stuck in traffic, she said, "No, he's not. I just saw him sitting in his car in the garage, talking on the phone – to you, I guess." Everybody laughed. Needless to say, when the exec hustled in a few minutes later, breathless, complaining about the horrible Ventura Freeway traffic, the rest of us experienced an embarrassingly bad entrance.

In improv, we take turns being the star and we do it onstage during a performance, as the circumstances of our scenes unfold. First and foremost, however, we are a team. One of the ways we show it is by supporting one another with timely entrances.

It should be noted that there are scenes in which a star turn can be appropriate. When one of your group is an acknowledged leader in your industry recently featured on the cover of *Fortune*, or if your audience is paying its money to see this star, it can be very effective for this person to make a big entrance when the stage is set. In fact, properly setting the stage for your 'Richard Branson' to enter builds audience anticipation, making the moment juicier and more effective for everybody involved. Here are some of the characteristics of good entrances:

Intention. Having a strong, clear sense of purpose when you enter a scene will naturally infuse your entrance with good energy. Your intention may be to initiate the scene with a fabulous gift to your scene partners, or it could be to support whatever's already happening in the scene. Whatever role you play, play it with clear intentions and 100% commitment from the first step, the first breath, the first words out of your mouth, the first click of the mouse.

Emotional Point of View. I cannot emphasize this enough. Maybe the single sagest piece of advice I've ever gotten from an improv teacher came from Jason Pardo, who demanded that his students enter and initiate scenes with conviction. Are you cheerful? Confident enough to conquer the world? Pragmatic? Eager? In business, when you enter with productive, positive emotions, scenes will get off the ground much more quickly and will have much more potential because your scene partners will pick up on your vibe. Other attributes of a good entrance will flow naturally from this conviction.

Good Energy. Your audience responds to and connects with your level of energy. Enter lethargically and filled with doubt and your audience will be lethargic right along with you and will doubt you doubly. On the other hand, bounce into a scene in high spirits and your audience will instantly be in a good mood. A positive, assertive level of energy also gives the scene a jolt from the get-go and becomes infectious within your team.

Timing. Timing is so important to improv comedy that a hesitation of half a second can mean the difference between a scene springing to life or falling flat. In business, we have a bit more time. Sometimes, a *lot* more time. Meetings can be scheduled weeks or months in advance. The important thing is, when the time comes, be there. Five minutes of lateness in business equates to that half-a-second of hesitation in comedy and can likewise be a difference-maker.

Exits

It's as simple as this: When it's time for you to get offstage, don't linger. Go. As with entrances, hesitant exits send a muddled message and indicate to the audience a lack of focus. With exits, the emphasis is not on making your presence felt but on removing yourself from the scene as if you're getting sucked offstage by a giant vacuum. Your energy all of a sudden belongs offstage, so let it take you there. Vanish! Evaporate! Vamoose! By making strong and definitive exits, you give 100% of the audience's attention to the entering player(s). Lollygagging and schmoozing with your business audience at the end of a scene can only dim whatever enthusiasm you've generated with your performance.

Additions

An addition happens when you join a scene in progress in order to bring useful information to it. Let's say your group is working on a bid for a project and you have intelligence on what your competitors are doing that the group will find helpful in making its bid. *All the characteristics of good entrances and exits apply to additions.* You want to add to a scene by entering and exiting well. Let's think about what that means.

First, get your timing right. If you have information like competitive intelligence that can inform the rest of the scene, you should enter when the information will have its biggest impact – in this case, at the beginning of the scene. Imagine if you add your analysis near end of the scene. It will potentially invalidate all the work that had been done prior. What a colossal waste of everyone's time! Timing your additions is part of the art.

Second, you want to add energetically. Don't let your additional information tiptoe into the scene; don't dribble it in little by little so that its impact is diminished or invisible. No – when it's time to go, get going with gusto! Get onstage and start adding information to the scene! Cue it up and connect!

Third, get in and get out. When you add to a scene, make a strong entrance and a clean exit. When you are not one of the central characters in the scene and your job is to support the central characters, add what you have to add, then exit. Let the group ask two or three questions, and then step aside so that the scene can resume with the focus on the central characters and the objective. Meetings can get completely derailed by an overload of sidebar information, which is why it's important to make additions brief. It helps maintain focus.

Edits

Edits are the moves made by players that mark the end of a scene and set the stage for the beginning of another. Current players exit and new ones enter. Players who edit skillfully have a knack for recognizing when scenes have reached their peak and can be concluded in a satisfying way. Skilled editing also comes into play when scenes have lost their focus and have strayed from the objective. In these situations, it's time to cut and move on, either to a scene with the same objective (if it was not achieved) or a scene with a new objective. Like additions, edits should be performed with the same techniques that characterize all good entrances and exits.

Here are three fundamentals to keep in mind in deciding when and how to edit your scenes:

Waste no time. The traffic patterns can get confusing on occasion, with players entering and exiting at the same time. Sort it out and keep up the energy. The millisecond one scene ends, the potential exits for a new one to begin.

During the construction of Disneyland, Walt Disney and a group of his company's executives flew into the Anaheim airport in a private plane during a rainstorm. Drenched while getting off the plane, they all sponged into a waiting sedan. And waited. Walt wanted to know what the delay was. They were waiting to give a ride to the pilot of the plane, explained one of his execs. At this information, Walt flew off the handle. Didn't anybody realize they had work to do?! He cussed them out like a Missouri farmer who just had a mule step on his foot, and didn't end his tirade until they reached the Disneyland construction site. Walt had no patience for poor edits between scenes. He wanted transitions between his business scenes to be as expertly edited as the ones in his films.

Give and take focus. Entering and exiting players should give and take focus strongly. When an edit is made, the entire group must support it. A scene cannot be partially edited. Editing a scene means that the entire group commits to the new focus and characters.

Edit at the peak. The very best time to edit a scene is when it has fully realized its potential to explore the objective. This is almost always marked by the peaking of energy and emotion. Editing at the peak not only gets the maximum impact out of the scene being edited, it helps transfer energy to the incoming scene. New characters get the benefit of 'drafting' off that energy to begin their new scenes.

V. COORDINATION

Of all the things I've done, the most vital is coordinating those

who work with me and aiming their efforts at a certain goal

— *Walt Disney*

ISSUES

IMPROV GROUPS HAVE *ISSUES*. Every group does. The issues often stem from the personal politics and drama that arise naturally within any group of people who spend a lot of time together. Ironically, the level of openness necessary to do good work can itself lead to issues within groups. It doesn't matter whether we're an improv troupe, the Indianapolis Colts or the Norfolk District at P & G. Our openness can connect and it can also wound. Stuff flares up. Romances flourish then crash, to the detriment of the group's psyche. Personal styles, sensibilities and frames of reference collide in slow motion, followed by slow motion destruction. The gossip flies. And all of it hampers, if not ruins, performances.

Improv groups, like every other living thing, have a natural life cycle. Some groups, cast well with people whose talents and personalities compliment one another, stay together for years. Other groups never make it out of rehearsals before they implode. The same kind of varying life spans should be expected of business groups. One would hope their demise results from professional growth and career movement of individuals in the group than because of relationships gone cataclysmically sour like in some sweeps week episode of *The Office* – but you never know. The personal space is full of perilous crosscurrents and eddies of emotion that must be navigated for the group to grow and stay productive throughout its natural life. And while we acknowledge that the personal space can be a crisis area for groups, and that it must be managed, this chapter is not about that, because those issues are not unique to improvisers. This chapter is about the issues that are unique to improvisers and what the improviser can do about them.

Most of the performance-related issues that teams and their members encounter are attributable to a less-than-stellar understanding or execution of the fundamentals described in *GameChangers*. Someone doesn't *Listen* well and misses an end-of-day deadline. Sloppy *Entrances and Edits* cause a presentation to drag. A lack of *Agreement* by your team alienates your audience. Lackluster performances can almost always be traced to poor fundamentals. By understanding the techniques and their potential, you become aware of the pitfalls and how to avoid them. Good improvisers and their coaches know that nearly every performance problem can be avoided with strong execution of the fundamentals. This mirrors John Wooden's philosophy when he was coaching basketball at UCLA. If the team is cast well and the fundamentals are executed with skill and conviction, the outcome of the game takes care of itself.

Common Issues

The issues detailed in this chapter comprise their own category of performance-related problems, all of which can be remedied by better execution of the fundamentals. GameChangers see these obstacles in the road from a mile away and veer around them or take another road altogether. The average improviser learns to swerve around these issues at the last second when confronted by them. Beginners run smack into them and suddenly find themselves in a ditch, wondering what hit them and how the wheels came off their scene.

Blocking. This is exactly what it sounds like – players impede the progress of a scene when they refuse the gifts offered to them by their teammates. Players who block say "Yes-but" or "No" instead of "Yes-and." Blocking occurs when players hijack a train of thought and try to spur it in their own self-interested direction. Scenes in which blocking occurs produce exchanges like:

> PLAYER 1: We're pushing a lot of chips on the table with this campaign.
>
> PLAYER 2: It's worth the investment.
>
> PLAYER 3: I bought a new lawn mower yesterday. *It* was worth the investment. That thing cuts quieter than my barber.

Player 3 blocks the progress of the scene. Players 1 and 2 set the pattern – risk analysis of a campaign. They are on their way to some kind of agreement about the direction the scene will take when Lawnmower Man derails the discussion, which will eventually require a restart to get back on track.

Certainly, many business scenarios have a healthy amount of skepticism associated with them. Our responsibilities as business-people include asking tough questions; to assess risk, you have to see the downside of a situation. Taken in a different context, blocking and parrying can both be advantageous business moves. But chronic blocking, in which the objective is obscured time and again, results in lost opportunities and lost productivity.

Denying. A form of blocking known as denying includes saying "no" a lot, and contradicting or ignoring other players, resulting in an ego-driven tug of war that confuses the audience more than any other issue. In improv theater, too much denying in a scene makes the audience ask themselves, "If they're confused up there, how am I supposed to know what's going on?" In business, it's exactly the same. No one will do business with a team that can't find agreement within itself. If agreement is the life's blood of improvisation, then denying is the Dracula that sucks the productivity out of scenes and the teamwork out of companies. Denying is what parents do to mis-behaving children – keeping them out of a scene they want to be in – not what business improvisers do to one another.

Fantasizing. All you need to build your scene is within you and your scene partners when the scene begins. It's still there in the mid-dle of the scene. It's there at the end. It is the reality you create together and share. It is the facts of the world you inhabit, whatever those facts are. A scene can only be built on what's with you in the moment. It's not about what will happen tomorrow, the next day, or in 50 years. It's not speculation about the actions of others who aren't in the scene. A scene is about you and me, here and now. When it comes to improvisation and business, you cannot say it to yourself often enough: *Don't invent what doesn't exist, deal with what does.*

Aaron Grosky, who negotiated hundreds of music and talent contracts for the *Live Earth* concerts staged around the world on July 7, 2007, says, "There's never been a concert like this before and prob-ably never will be again. We're not making it up as we go along. If we were making it up, that would mean we were imagining it, not living in reality. If we want this to happen, we have to act on what's real. What's right in front of us. What's next." There could be no better description than Grosky's on the hazards of fantasizing, no better testament to the importance of working in reality than the massive music and talent roster assembled around the planet for *Live Earth*.

Flatlining. When the players in a scene show no kick, no energy or life, the scene will be DOA. It will not have a chance. Strong, committed choices bring players and their scenes to life. A strong choice is a gift to the other players on your team. Think about a presentation as a typical business scene staged by a team of people. When you, as a player on that team, make a strong choice – in the form of your enthusiasm, your knowledge of the subject matter, your helpfulness in getting the presentation on its feet – you give a gift to your teammates that will last for the life of the scene. If you go in flat, reserved and non-committal, you are saying a lot about how you feel about the scene, your scene partners and your audience – none of it good.

Going to Crazy Town. This is my teacher Michael Bertrando's phrase for when the invention and fantasizing in a scene get out of hand, until the scene becomes un-moored from any comprehensible frame of reference. In improv theater, a scene that goes to Crazy Town will spin up exchanges like:

PLAYER 1: You're not from around here.

PLAYER 2: No, I'm from the planet Chipotle.

PLAYER 3: Then I'll have to shoot you with my salsa ray.

In three lines, we have an alien from a planet named for Mexican food getting zapped with a dip gun. In three more lines, we'll be on a spaceship made of tortillas bound for a moon made of guacamole. Trust me, I've seen it happen often enough to know.

A business scene that goes to Crazy Town might spawn an exchange like this:

PLAYER 1: By offering our customers an improved product with a brand new name, we will change the market.

PLAYER 2: Change the market? We'll dominate it!

PLAYER 3: Who's talking about the market? We're going to change the world!

Ah, yes. Another titanic moment in the history of products that are going to change the world. Sales pitches, even ones that don't get all the way to Crazy Town, frequently get lost in its suburbs. Good business gets conducted on the facts, not the hype. So does good improvisation. Going to Crazy Town is different from the fantasizing issue in that it tends to be related to an unrealistic objective.

Back in the dotcom era, we spent a lot of time in Crazy Town. I personally heard pitches and read business plans for things like a federally funded robotic crop picking project that was being re-envisioned as a 3-D web browser; another backed by "New Zealand tourism money" for a plan to webcast the Sydney Olympics by pirating the NBC satellite feed from the rooftop of a hotel near Sydney Stadium; and still another for online auctions of property confiscated from drug dealers. As a member of the audience for these pitches, I felt that the performers were taking me to worlds that only they understood, one that nothing in my own experience would lead me to believe. People who consistently play in Crazy Town – how can you help but think they're anything but crazy?

Grandstanding. Players who are always trying to make *the* killer move in a scene fall victim to this issue. Remember this: The killer move can only be killer in retrospect, never ahead of time. Looking for it to happen doesn't help it happen; in fact, it makes it less likely that it will, because it disconnects you from the scene and the group. Grandstanders spend so much time and effort awaiting the perfect opportunity to bring an awesome move to the scene that they're constantly holding back instead of engaging in what's happening in the moment. They are concerned about the before ("When will my time come?") and after ("What will people say?") of the scene but never the 'now'. Grandstanding behaviors in business scenes include waiting to be the last person to speak on any given subject (the 'Here Come Da Judge' game), namedropping, angry tirades, especially when they're directed at the group or one of its members, and dominating the dialogue.

Interrogation. Anyone who's ever taken an improv class has been taught that questions are an impediment to good scene work. As with most rules and guidelines about improvisation, this one's not ironclad. Can you ask questions in a scene and still have it be good? Yes, you can. "Learn the rules so you can forget them," says Jason Pardo. "The rules are more diagnostic than predictive. They tell us more about why a scene went bad than about how to make a good one."

Generally speaking, business improvisers should not hold back from asking pertinent questions in their scenes. We *have* to ask questions, it's an obligation. That's why I call this issue interrogation. When a player does nothing but ask questions, the give-and-take goes only one way, which means the scene will not build, and the relationship in the scene will not grow or change. The game becomes one of extracting information, which is not improvisation. Improvisation is *doing something* with information. Friendly interrogation is a form of blocking; skeptical or hostile interrogation, a way of denying.

Judging. When you're in a scene, you think that it sucks, you lose enthusiasm for it and you start to wish you were somewhere else – that's judging. Don't do it. Instead, make something happen. *Double* your commitment. Judging is subjective. It's your ego talking, it's your head getting the best of your instincts, which is not where you want to be. To avoid judging, support your teammates. Find something small and make it bigger, or something big and shrink it. Find a piece of information and add to it. It will keep you in the game. You can decide later if you and the scene sucked. During the scene is not the time.

Justifying. Explaining why everything is the way it is and how it got to be that way – sometimes referred to as exposition, other times as making excuses, and still other times as scapegoating – stops a scene in its tracks. When you begin to draw extraneous information into the scene with the idea of bolstering your position or blaming others for problems you have to solve, what you're often doing instead is losing focus. If you are connected through the group mind, you do not have to justify anything or blame anyone. To a player who addresses the reality agreed to and shared by the group, everything is justified and no one is to blame. Things simply are the way they are. The group deals with that, never what might have been.

Pandering. In improv theater, this is known as 'going for the easy laugh'. In business, it's known as, well, pandering. The form of pandering most familiar to business people is the kickback or bribe. It can also take the form of advertising that skirts any real description of your product and appeals instead to some baser instinct of the audience. Promises of miracles to your audience – like getting rich overnight or losing 20 pounds in a month while eating all you want – that's pandering. It's a way of getting the audience's attention without earning it. In general, you're not doing your audience, be they customers, clients or fellow employees, any favors by pandering. The appeal is highly transitory. Perhaps pandering is an effective technique for con artists and fly-by-nighters, but it's no way to build a brand that the world will believe in.

Pimping. This is probably much more of an issue on the improv theater stage than it is in business, but it deserves a mention. When, during a scene, you make an unreasonable demand or set unreasonable expectations for one of your fellow players, you're pimping them. You direct a fellow player to perform a lewd act on another. That's pimping, in multiple senses of the word. You label someone a musical genius and then ask that player to sing a Gilbert and Sullivan operetta. Unless you really do expect the player to know the lyrics, you're pimping. The equivalent in business – often known as 'throwing somebody under the bus' – would be to put a fellow employee in an impossible situation by promising the audience what you know they cannot deliver. When you tell a client on Tuesday, "Jeremy can have the API layer written by the end of the week," knowing that Jeremy is at a conference until Thursday, you're pimping Jeremy. Don't do it. Give gifts instead. Help makes things possible for your teammates, not impossible.

Scripting. When you have the entire scene written out in your mind (or anywhere else, for that matter) before it begins and expect the subsequent scene to stick to that script, you're going to end up in the ditch. The very definition of improvisation dictates the terms – no script. It isn't easy to rid ourselves of preconceptions and expectations, yet we have to if we are to achieve the objective. Scripts are subjective and freighted with ego. No one can see what we're thinking and so, when we 'script', the ensuing scene will usually dissolve into a disagreement between players, confusion from the audience, or both. In business, scripting often means we're trying to promote our own personal agenda or achieve an outcome we've decided ahead of time.

To avoid scripting, enter scenes with a single strong idea about the role you're playing, nothing more; and instead of your own performance, focus on supporting your teammates. If you find yourself with a script in your head, burn it before the scene begins. Goals are good. Deciding ahead of time that there's only way to achieve them is not.

Turning Mistakes Into Gold

Shulie Cowen encourages players in her classes at I.O. West to turn their mistakes into gold: "Don't try too hard to fix them," she says. "Look at them as an opportunity to create understanding and clarity where there is none."

Andy Lipkis, founder of the L.A.-based nature conservancy, Tree People, puts it like this: "Failure is the compost of success."

What is true for improv groups is also true for business organizations. The story of human endeavor is the story of how failure is the forerunner to success. Libraries of books have been written about it, so I won't belabor the obvious here, except to say that comebacks are always great for audiences, whether it's the audience in a theater or your customer audience. I myself experienced this first-hand when I observed and participated in the resurgence of the The Walt Disney Company from the early-1980s to the mid-1990s. From a storytelling standpoint, failure is not a bad place to be, as long as you believe firmly in the inevitability of your success.

As an improviser, you have the skills to merit faith – your own and that of others – in your eventual success. You welcome your missteps because they help you define more productive paths and profitable directions for your scenes. When you're in a scene and you see that it's floundering, you know how to make a move that will send it in a better direction, and in so doing, sow the seeds of your success.

Here are techniques for getting out of trouble when you're in it:

Move. It's hard to talk your way out of trouble, but movement can carry you away from the issue and into a fresh idea.

Embrace it. What looks like a problem may, in fact, be a sign that you're not going far enough. It sounds obvious, but you'd be surprised how many times we label a situation as troublesome when it's simply an underperformed scene. In other words…if what you're doing isn't selling, maybe you're not doing it enough. Try doing it more.

Simplify. Focus on doing one thing really well. Pare down what the scene is about and get at the most important thing.

Use emotion. Get your dander up. Be kind, generous or even controversial. If a lack of engagement in the objective is the issue, emotion can help sharpen focus.

Seduce. Elaine May famously said, "When in doubt, seduce." This does not mean coming onto an attractive coworker, but engaging your scene partners in the enjoyment of playing the game. Let's say we have a crushing deadline ahead of us. If the focus is not on the deadline, but on our collaboration as its own reward, that's seductive stuff. Seduction heightens the involvement of the players. It never gets old or stale and can help almost any scene. It is a move for all seasons.

Shulie Cowan's husband, Kai Narezo, a professional musician, says, "The good news about bad notes is that there's always a good one right next to them."

When the business improviser makes a mistake, he or she smiles knowing that the reward is right around the corner.

Follow the Fear

"Follow the fear" is a famous improv aphorism coined by the legendary teacher, Del Close. As with a lot of improv teaching that came out of Chicago from the 1930s through the 1970s, this saying says a lot about life.

"All we have to fear is fear itself," said Franklin D. Roosevelt.

"Sooner or later, you have to do the thing that scares you most," the humorist and radio performer, Garrison Keillor (paraphrasing Mark Twain) said to me one day on the front porch of his house in St. Paul, Minnesota. Keillor was referring to his own success as an author and radio host, but he could have been talking about anyone in business…or in improvisation for that matter. Fear is a closed door. On the other side of that door is the success you cannot currently imagine, residing there as the potential of your subconscious mind. To achieve that success, you must open the door and walk through.

Let's face it, most of us are scared to get up in front of other people and perform. And many of us, especially those of us in a corporate environment, fear the business move that will put us onstage and expose our behaviors as being noteworthy or unique in some way. Yet this is necessary if we are to break through and create new wealth from new ideas.

Perhaps your own fears are tied up in issues of security. You are afraid of jeopardizing the comfort and security of what you have today in order to reach the tomorrow you dream about. Well, you know what? There are no guarantees about tomorrow. Your dreams and expectations of security both exist in the realm of unrealized possibilities. So why not reach for your dreams?

To overcome your fear, go right at the fear. You hear professional athletes talk about facing their fears when they are in a major competition with the eyes of the world on them. How do they do it? First, they *trust*. They trust the fundamentals of their game. They trust instincts honed from years of experience in other pressure-filled situations. And in team sports, they trust their teammates. They do not try to guide the outcome, but work with confidence that the outcome will be good.

Second, they have *desire* – it means that they're passionate about their performance. It means something to them. It defines who they are and what they're made of.

Finally, they have *courage*. Courageous behavior comes about when, motivated by our desire, someone follows their fear and faces it. It is said that great performers 'rise' to a challenge. Notice that nobody ever says a great performer shrinks to the challenge. Greatness comes with stepping forward, not retreating.

For businesspeople, following your fear often means defying conventions and the expectations of others. Like stellar performances in the athletic arena, following the unmarked trail that leads to new prosperity takes trust in the fundamentals, a burning desire to achieve one's goals and the courage to act on those desires.

Business people do not stay in business long if they're foolhardy. Fearlessness does not mean recklessness. Risks must be assessed. And there's no dishonor in a conservative approach, if the risks outweigh the rewards. But recognize that your potential as player resides in what you don't yet know about yourself, but are bold enough to discover. Discover it by focusing on the game and the fundamentals of improvisation. If you have the gumption to open the door, they will see you through to the other side.

COACHING

IN IMPROVISATION, THE TITLES 'COACH' AND 'DIRECTOR' are used interchangeably for the person who gives guidance to a team. In *GameChangers*, we call it *Coaching* and those who do it *coaches* so as not to create unnecessary confusion with the typical business title of Director. Furthermore, those with the title of Director in an organization should not be confused with people who coach improvisers. Even those who work as directors in the theatrical realm are not always good coaches. Coaching improvisers is its own discipline, one as rigorous and essential to team success as any other in the curriculum. Coaching, as defined by *GameChangers*, amalgamates the talents of athletic coaches, teachers and theatrical directors, and orients those talents toward business. The coach serves many roles and performs many functions that are vital to the chemistry of the team. This chapter will define and describe the skills that go into good coaching. It is important for the improvisational organization to: recognize the individuals within its ranks who have the natural talent and inclination to become good coaches; and encourage managers to focus on the skills that make good coaches (yes, your Directors are finally going to learn how to direct). Without coaching, teams cannot realize their potential any more than a caterpillar can fly.

Why coaches are necessary. As an improviser, you need someone telling you what he or she sees in your performance. But the 'seeing' done by coaches involves more than the visual. Coaching is the mirror held up to the improviser's senses, instincts and emotions. Improvising without a coach, especially in rehearsals and run-throughs, can be a chaotic affair, filled with conflicting opinions and a lack of focus. In these situations, when there are typically many different items on the agenda, the coach keeps the scene moving and the team focused on its objective.

Even the most talented players need coaching and sometimes they need it the most. Big talent left unchecked and unguided will rocket in every random direction like somebody dropped a match into a box full of fireworks. Egos collide. People get hurt. If you don't want your most talented players becoming your most destructive personalities, coach them well. In business, good managers have the ability to channel a team's energy into productive areas, and eliminate the noise and distractions that diminish productivity. As organizations adapt and evolve in the Networked World, our ideas about managing business teams will have to adapt and evolve, too. Good coaching is essential to this process.

Casting. In the Industrial Age, professional athletes typically played their entire careers with one organization and the working public did likewise. Teams were cast in steel and stone. In the Networked World, with free agency a way of life, teams change rosters on a regular basis. This means that casting has become a more important skill than ever before. Managers stuck in the industrial mindset will find the fluidity of a team's identity to be a burden, as each change in the roster brings with it a new set of challenges that didn't exist before. Managers geared to the networked way of working see this fluidity as an opportunity, because casting well is one of their skills.

Casting can come about through hiring new employees or tapping existing employees for new assignments. It does not necessarily mean giving promotions, although some new roles give a player a higher status than his or her former role. In casting, what's foremost in the coach's mind is the concept of the team. What mix of skills, personalities, energies and interests will lead to the most productive performance?

Billions of words have been written about putting together productive teams, but no one can sum it up better than the legendary basketball coach (and teacher), John Wooden, who said, "I play my best five, not my five best." Improvisation coaches recognize individual talents and integrate them accordingly to form the best team.

Teaching. The opportunity to learn in the workplace is important to an individual's growth and success in the Networked World, and is a major factor in employee job satisfaction. A good coach acts as a teacher to the team. Not only will the coach be well versed in the techniques of business improvisation and knowledgeable about the business itself, he or she will be adept at creating opportunities for team learning. In improvisation, the teacher does not teach in the pedantic sense, but guides students down pathways to learning. "Open that door," says the coach-as-teacher to the team. "Walk through it. Your learning resides on the other side."

Coaching-as-teaching does not mean saddling people with scads of useless information. It does not require heavy bouts of rote memorization. Rather, the coach-as-teacher understands how the team dynamic can create 'learning scenes'. In these scenes, team members will come to a couple of realizations: Scenes benefit from useful information, and the more knowledge you have, the stronger you'll be as a player. A good coach, in explaining how and why business scenes work improvisationally, illuminates the paths to knowledge that team members will find valuable to both their scenes and their careers. "Knowledge," says the coach-as-teacher to the team, "makes you a better player. Better players make better scenes. Better scenes make better business." With that understanding in place, learning becomes a byproduct of good coaching and good teamwork. The improvisational organization thrives on learning and succeeds because of it.

Observation. "Oh wad some power the giftie gie us, To see oursels as others see us!" wrote the poet Robert Burns in the poem *To a Louse.* This is the 'giftie' coaches give their teams: They tell us what they see and, in doing so, help us see ourselves as others see us. Most of us have misconceptions about how we are seen by others. Remember the first time you heard your voice on a recording or saw yourself on video? Who was *that?* Seeing ourselves, being observed and having observations made about us is not everyone's cup of tea. Get over it. If you are in business, you are visible in the world, and it helps to have that visibility described to us in terms that are constructive and beneficial to the cause. By making observations within the context of improvisation techniques, a good coach helps alleviate some of the sensitivities that come with personal criticism.

The current generation of employees entering the workplace is more open to being observed than generations past, chiefly because it is the most observed generation in history. From birth, 'Gen-Why?' has been MySpaced, FaceBooked and YouTubed ad nauseum. There aren't a lot of surprises left in terms of physical appearance. We are talking about people who know how they look and what they sound like. What they don't know and cannot see is how they improvise. How they perform. This is where coaching comes in. The misconceptions we have about ourselves may be subtler as we get more experienced in the world, but it doesn't mean we don't still have them.

One of the most valuable types of observations a coach can make is the effect we have versus the effect we intend. Do we communicate our intentions clearly? Do our emotions manifest themselves as positive, productive behaviors? By carefully noting the actions of a team and comparing those actions to intentions, the coach reduces the ambiguity and misunderstanding that arise in everyday business dialogue.

COACH: You brought up Buffalo when we were talking about the Sacramento market. Why?

PLAYER: I wanted to show them how we performed in a similar market.

COACH: You didn't say that.

PLAYER: I didn't?

COACH: No.

PLAYER: I thought I did.

COACH: You might have thought it, but you didn't say it. It seemed as if you were trying to change the subject

PLAYER: I wasn't.

COACH: I know that. They didn't know that.

Other kinds of observations made by coaches include identifying missed opportunities, assessing the effectiveness of communication between players on a team, the timing of edits made during a scene, and the team's success at achieving the objective.

Defining the objective. In improv theater, 'the objective' describes a state of mind, a place outside oneself that transcends ego, personal judgment and the everyday world. When the objective is achieved, a universe in its entirety exists on the stage, spun into existence by the improvisational activities of the players, with the audience swept along for the ride.

As defined by *GameChangers*, the objective state relates more to the business purpose of the scene. When we speak of 'achieving the objective' in business improvisation, we do not necessarily refer to a transcendent experience but instead to a world that orbits around a business-related *raison d'etre*. Examples of everyday business objectives are a budget, a campaign, a contract dispute, a job interview, etc. Achieving the objective, in these examples, means players find agreement through the objective. Even if the agreement does not consist of settling the contract dispute or getting hired for the job, it brings about a common ground on which the scene partners can agree. This is the objective state a coach will help players achieve through practiced and disciplined focus.

Skilled coaches guide their teams toward objectives by getting players to make productive moves and by steering them away from dead ends. To use a basic example, a good coach will not let a scene turn jokey. Too much jokiness obscures the objective. So while it's good to laugh and get laughs, it's almost never the reason a business objective is achieved. Another example of an unproductive avenue for a scene is a game we'll call 'My Kids Love It'. The prescient charm of your children, your wife, your wife's yoga instructor or your rich uncle is undeniable, but it is not a fair game to cite them as reliable market research, or to pay more respect to their ideas than to those of the players in your group. The coach is the person in the best position to remind everyone of this and not ruffle any feathers.

I was once in a business meeting in Los Angeles that unexpectedly ran through lunch. One person, something of a status-obsessed prima donna, wanted to order wine. Fine. A nearby restaurant faxed over a menu and its wine list. The prima donna grabbed the wine list and began studying it intently. Meanwhile, the meeting proceeded and everyone passed around a piece of paper on which they wrote their lunch orders. That piece of paper somehow bypassed the wine-list-obsessed prima donna and the lunch order got phoned in without his order on it. When the prima donna realized that everyone but him had ordered lunch, he blew a gasket. Then he sulked. For the rest of the meeting, through his belated lunch and beyond, he did not contribute a single worthwhile thought. If there had been someone in that meeting in a coaching role, the lunch with wine would not have become the focus. But that is what happened and productivity suffered badly because of it. The prima donna had big talent and his non-participation hurt.

Coaching during performances. Unlike coaches in improv theater, coaches of business teams have the opportunity to coach during performances. No one wants to see their coach overdo it with direction in front of an audience, but subtle cues, segues and gestures that contextualize the presentation can be very helpful to the team.

Coaching rehearsals and run-throughs. In business, many types of scenes cannot be completely improvised. They have to have an agenda and a certain amount of buy-in from the scene partners ahead of time. When this is the case, rehearsals are often advisable or necessary. During rehearsals, coaches play dual roles, assessing the team's work from both the constructive view of an ally and the critical view of the audience. They appraise a performance for total running time, tempo, flow and editing, among other criteria. They make sure the client's needs are addressed. They give the team its ways and reasons for raising emotions in the context of its performance. In rehearsals and run-throughs, the coach of a business team performs precisely the same role as a coach in improv theater.

Reading the audience. The greatest talent of some coaches (and what often what makes them great managers) is that they can read an audience like a Vegas headliner taking the pulse of a capacity showroom crowd. They are adept at addressing both the letter and the spirit of a client's RFP, for example. They know what the hot buttons will be in a presentation. They identify decision makers and decision-making processes. They get their team in a place to appeal to the customer's emotions as well as their pocketbooks.

Contextualizing. The coach helps a team connect its scenes to the bigger picture. He or she does it primarily by using metaphor. For many business scenes, the metaphor used by the coach will be the organization's brand. You see this kind of 'contextual coaching' done in any organization – from Mountain Dew to the Mormon Tabernacle Choir – that has a strong sense of its own identity. I once had Mountain Dew as a client and it was all about being a little bit nuts in your thinking and, of course, your actions. 'Extreme' was the name of the game. The board was the metaphor. Skateboard. Snowboard. Surfboard. Never bored. A coach involved in scenes with Mountain Dew would be wise to remind his team of the brand's extreme sports metaphors in everything it does. The best brands work with metaphors that resonate right down to the very core of the organization. The best coaches keep those metaphors alive in their teams' performances.

Establishing environment. Whenever possible, coaches help establish environments for their teams' scenes that are conducive to achieving the objective. In improv theater, building the environment falls to the players. The coach can guide them during rehearsals, but once a performance begins, players are on their own to build environments on the blank canvases of the empty stage and the audience's expectant imaginations. In business, the furniture and the food are real. Their affect on players and audience is likewise real. Cubicles have a different feeling and have a different effect on players than bullpens. A room with comfortable couches sets the stage for a different kind of scene than a room with metal folding chairs. A coffee shop scene is a different scene than a Happy Hour scene. The wise coach recognizes the effect environment can have, and helps the team schedule and work in the spaces most conducive to the business activity that will transpire in them.

Evaluation. At the end of rehearsals and after performances, it is the responsibility of the coach to lead an evaluation of the team's work. Evaluations are important to the growth and improvement of a group. As Viola Spolin, the godmother of modern improv, writes in her classic text, *Improvisation for the Theater,* "It is time to establish objective vocabulary, and direct communication made possible through non-judgmental attitudes, group assistance in solving a problem and clarification of the focus." Did the team members keep their focus? How did they meet the challenges they faced? Did they communicate well? Did they perform with good energy? When a coach evaluates according to the precepts of the techniques, the group regards the evaluation as integral to their discovery of the truth about their work and about themselves.

VI. Preceding Success

I find my greatest pleasure, and so my reward,

in the work that precedes what the world calls success.

— *Thomas Alva Edison*

JOB INTERVIEWS

NO BUSINESS ACTIVITY HAS MORE TO GAIN from the improvisational model than the *Job Interview*. Job interviews are typically pro-forma. They feel scripted, because they usually are. The interviewer either adheres to a reference document called something like 'The Seven Questions of Highly Effective Recruiters' or they follow a company-recommended guideline. Given the frequency with which most companies interview prospective employees, and the constraints of time, money and imagination on people doing the interviewing, these scenes almost *have* to follow a script. The problem with the scene is that the interviewee knows the script just as well as the interviewer. Any job candidate worth their salt has answers to all the stock questions. Because of this, nothing gets revealed. You can judge a candidate's appearance and his or her technical prowess, but in the scenario described above, it's hard to know what the *experience* of working with that candidate is going to be. And that working experience is vital to a company's culture and, ultimately, to the life of its brand. You can have the most knowledgeable workforce in the world, but if they're impossible to work with – if they 'know it all' – who's going to want to do business with your company?

In this chapter, we're going to look at how to change the game that gets played in most job interviews. You go from having multiple scripts and stock answers for a job interview to having none. In having no script, no stock answers, you liberate the opportunity for each interview to become its own scene, its own experience. You allow yourself to see the intentions of the characters in the scene. You honor individuality.

In the Industrial Age, job interviews were designed to assure the interviewer and the organization that a candidate could adequately fill a well-defined role. Candidates were like actors auditioning for well-known plays. The script had already been written and the roles defined by a generation of actors who'd played them before. Nobody wanted any surprises. They may have *said* they wanted surprises. They did not. And then, suddenly – surprise! – things changed. From an ideal of 'filling a well-defined role', the new ideal for an employee has become 'creating a role that didn't exist before we hired you'.

In the Networked World, your quest is to continually present yourself – your talent, business, product and brand – to your audience as a unique value proposition. 'Sameness', in the form of repetition, standardization or doctrinaire behavior, doesn't look to your audience like you're sitting pretty, it looks like you're moving backward in a hurry. Solidity and structure have taken a backseat to transparency and fluidity. The improvisational job interview is designed to appeal to, and reveal, the players flexible and open enough to play the new game.

A friend of mine who works for a Fortune 500 company once complained to me about employees with glowing academic credentials but little real business experience. "I have all these educated idiots on my team," he said. *Educated idiots!* The phrase stuck with me. Anyone experienced with the Networked World will know what he's talking about. The rote learning you acquired in B-school does not guarantee success in today's marketplace. Which is not to say you didn't learn anything in school or that what you learned won't be useful. But what you need to know to be a real player cannot be guaranteed by a diploma. You need to be as confident in your human instincts as you are in your book smarts. One without the other is not much good. Your business scenes will be much more productive, and your themes can be explored more thoroughly, when real world experience and a formal education are *both* in play.

Notes for Job Candidates

We live in an age when everybody knows a lot, and what we don't know is just a mouse-click away. What matters is how we put our knowledge to use. The improvisational job interview allows a candidate to demonstrate competencies that will help them become strong players in the new business world:

Creativity. In the improvisational business, creativity resides everywhere, not just in the Creative department. It manifests itself as 'playfulness with the material'. It doesn't matter whether that material is used for administration or to generate intellectual properties; whether your game is finance or project management. In business, 'playing' used to mean screwing around with the books, insider trading, having an affair with an intern or just plain goofing-off on company time. Today, play is not a business pejorative. It is a prerequisite for excellence. Having a company with a creative culture means sharing a sense of exhilaration about the day-to-day life of the business you're in, about the new ideas that keep it vibrant and competitive. Creativity means you're making things happen more than things are happening to you. You make moves that excite your audience. You champion good ideas. Creativity knows no boundaries between personal and professional lives. Self-expression, after all, is self-expression, wherever it happens. People who live creatively work creatively and vice versa. The source of it all is play. If there's one thing the improvisational job interview does phenomenally well, it's bringing playfulness to light.

Character. Character is shorthand for a lot of virtues and, to most improvisational companies, it's probably the trait that matters most. Stripped of the title, the salary, the resume, the wardrobe, the references, who is this candidate? What matters to them? Do they have the ability to laugh at themselves? Are they resilient? Open? Authentic? Is their energy consistent with that of your organization?

Alertness. This doesn't relate to how many cups of coffee the candidate pounds every morning. No, this kind of alertness describes a person's ability to walk through life with eyes wide open. What's on their radar and how did it get there? A business, like any other organism, has senses. It sees. It hears. It touches. You get a sense from the second you walk into a company's lobby what kind of taste it has. The networked organization bundles the nerve endings and sensibilities of its employees into what we could call its brand personality. It needs players with sharp and alert sensibilities, people who have a good ear for useful information, people who pay attention to what's happening in the world around them. *The impro-visational business does not hire people who share its sensibilities, but people with sensibilities worth sharing.* Employees who bring different perspectives to their scenes make those scenes powerful and productive. A thousand perspectives, shared, yield one hell of an organizational worldview. A rubber-stamped perspective, shared a thousand times, gives you the world seen through a pinhole.

Flexibility. A candidate's flexibility should mirror the flexible nature of the networked organization. This flexibility manifests itself as agile thinking, the ability to resolve paradox, the courage and confidence to work 'outside the manual' toward fresh solutions, and the resourcefulness to roll with the daily punches and quickly turn mistakes into progress.

Persistence. We need dreams. And we need the persistence to pursue them purposefully and energetically. A job interview can articulate a candidate's dreams as well as professional aspirations. So what if those dreams aren't going to be realized in the job or even in the company to which you're applying? No big deal. Companies do not exist to make dreams come true. They exist to exist tomorrow, and the next day, and on into the future. What we want to know, as job candidates, is that every one our days spent with an organization will move us, in some way, a little closer to our dreams. What we want to know when we hire somebody is that they're going to play with the kind of energy that can only come from a person with ambitions about the world.

Boldness. The next generation of employees has been gifted with a set of communications tools that are changing the world. This is not a time for shrinking violets. Who has the boldness to be heard, the forthrightness to make their mark with these tools? These are the employees companies are looking for, because they take action. They make choices. They give a sense of *movement* to an organization.

Problem Solving. Let us not forget to honor those who have the knack for bringing form and logic to their scenes. It's great to be creative and dream big, but it's all for naught if that energy isn't directed toward solving a problem or reaching a goal. Problem-solvers simplify complex situations. Even if the interviewer doesn't pose an immediate problem in the course of the interview, the candidate should, wherever possible, demonstrate adroitness at problem-solving.

Sense of Humor. In business, as in life, sometimes the only thing you can do at the end of a rough day is laugh. People with the ability to approach difficult scenes with a sense of humor – not necessarily with the objective of making anyone laugh, but with good spirits and a smile – lighten the load for everyone. Having a sense of humor warms up your audience and gives it a rooting interest in your fate. And it shows the interviewer that you're not just a list of credentials on your resumé, you also have a healthy perspective on the world.

Discretion. There's a reason why it's the better part of valor. It is up to the interviewee to feel out what is most appropriate for the scene. Is the interviewer tired? Distracted? Did your witty remark get a laugh, or fall flat? The quicker you can get a 'read' on the other person or people in the room, the sooner you can begin bridging the distance between the job interview and the job offer.

Notes for Interviewers

How do you conduct or give an improvisational job interview? You treat the interview as an unscripted performance:

Set the environment. Where you conduct your interviews says a lot about your company and what you want to get out of the scene. An interview in a windowless office with a closed door will be an entirely different interview than one conducted with the same person while taking a walk around the block or hitting golf balls at a driving range.

Have an audience. This may be the single biggest difference between a job interview in the Industrial Age, and one in the Networked World. It is very difficult for people in the scene to observe the scene, so others should be present if possible. Whether it's during the interview itself, or whether you add audience while the scene is in progress (i.e. have the candidate meet fellow employees), it is important that people other than those in the scene observe the scene. How does the candidate respond to suggestions from the audience? What does the scene look like to the audience? What is revealed? What transformations occur? Does a relationship form? What happens in the scene that reveals a candidate's character?

Develop characters. As with any improvised scene, the improvisational job interview should define its characters in detail. The work of the interviewer is not only to help the candidate reveal his or her true colors, but for the interviewer to reveal his or her personality as well. Defining characters in detail opens the door to a relationship between those characters.

Build relationships. The proposal underpinning all job interviews is the proposal of a relationship between the interviewee and the people in the hiring company. It's not a relationship between a person and a company, but *a relationship between people.* Whatever relationship develops in the interview suggests one that could develop between the candidate and people in the hiring company. Candidates cannot demonstrate their skill in relationship building unless the interviewer opens up to it and stages the interview scene accordingly.

Replace questions with statements. The call and response pattern that characterizes most job interviews has bastardized the very word 'interview'. We generally define the term as one person asking questions of the other. But the word 'interview' comes from the French *entrevue*, meaning 'to see each other'. What a wonderfully improvisational meaning that is. I am seriously tempted to redefine what happens between candidate and interviewer as an 'entreview', but for the purpose of sharing a common frame of reference, we'll stick to the familiar term but return to its root meaning: to see each other.

"What would you say are your greatest strengths?" the interviewer asks in a traditional call-and-response interview. (Candidate names strengths.) "What's something you'd like to get better at?" (Candidate lists areas for improvement.) "Where do you see yourself in five years?" (Candidate paints rosy future calculated to be slightly less rosy than the future of the interviewer.) And then the interviewer asks, "Are there any questions you'd like to ask me?" (Candidate asks a tough-but-not-so-tough-as-to-stump-the-interviewer question.) This kind of paint-by-numbers scene will result in a pretty, but predictable, picture. The candidate you *want* to hire paints a picture you haven't seen before.

In business, we are given raw material, often in the form of information, and are expected to add value to that material. Questioning candidates is not providing them with information they can act on, it is a request for information the *interviewer* can act on. In this dynamic, the candidate is not seen acting on information, as in a real working scenario. By making declarative, information-rich statements, the interviewer takes the scene out of the past or future, and into the present. When a scene is in the present, it cannot help but be active. The most enlightening job interviews, those most likely to result in an excellent hire, build scenes that reveal how well the candidate plays the game.

Interview Games

So...how do you know what games to play? To that, I give you the same answer I'd give any beginning improviser before a performance: You don't know. The scene's participants determine what games are played *while the scene is happening*. This is not to say that you cannot have games in your repertoire. In improv comedy, there are dozens of games that, over the past half-century, have become part of the lexicon of the technique. Name a game like 'Town Meeting', 'Living Room', or 'Build a Product' for any experienced improviser and they'll know exactly what game you're talking about, and can play it, no questions asked. What's also true is that none of those experienced improvisers will feel as if a performance has realized its potential through the playing of a timeworn game. The joy of improvisation comes with discovering a game you've never played before. So it is with job interviews. You can and should develop games to have in your repertoire; more importantly, you should always be aware of the opportunities in the moment to play a game that will reveal something relevant about the candidate. The really rich, rewarding stuff awaits discovery in the course of the interview.

Here are some improvisational games my clients, business acquaintances and I myself have played to good effect during job interviews.

Good Cop, Bad Cop. This is a game that's often played when two interviewers conduct the interview. One of them begins in a typical Q & A style, with softball questions lobbed at the candidate in an easygoing, predictable rhythm. When this cordial rhythm has been established, second interviewer walks in late and turns the interview upside down. Asks questions and interrupts before the candidate can complete an answer. Changes the tempo and energy of the scene. The second interviewer might be nervous, in a hurry, borderline obnoxious, or slow and stupid. He might disagree with a candidate's opinions or pick a fight with the other interviewer. The candidate's capacity to play this game reveals poise, the ability to react gracefully under pressure, a sense of humor and presence of mind. Even if the candidate catches on that the interviewers are role-playing, an adaptive personality will play along. Good Cop, Bad Cop reveals players who react well to stressful situations. For high-pressure jobs like project management and sales, this can be a very constructive interview game.

The Ride-Along. Many people, especially in sales, play this game as part of the interview process. My feeling is that it has become something of a cliché. Candidate hops in car with Sales Manager, goes with Sales Manager on sales calls while the two of them get to know one another. Sales Manager extols virtues of the company, describes the job opening and what's expected of the candidate. Candidate tries to get along with the Sales Manager and demonstrate a take-charge attitude despite being cast in the relatively passive role of riding shotgun. The problem with this game is that it's time-worn. Everyone knows it. The roles are defined. It's as familiar to interviewers and candidates as *Death of a Salesman* is to Broadway performers. Not that it isn't a meaty play. It is. But it's not the kind of play that energizes a savvy improviser. The improviser's advantage comes with creating variations on The Ride-Along.

Tamara Sibson, CEO of Physicians Health, Inc., founded her company in April, 2007. Using *GameChangers* techniques, she is building a networked organization that is extremely fluid and improvisational. She does not look to cast employees who tell her what she already knows about Physicians Health, but for those who can communicate and act on their own vision for the company. Here's her challenge as an interviewer: Because Physicians Health has an extremely complex infrastructure requiring 71 hand-offs of information per transaction, she cannot expect potential employees to immediately grasp the intricacies of the offering, enough to offer a relevant vision of their own. So that's not her game. In Sibson's version of The Ride-Along, she will initiate a scene that *explores the theme of vision.* For example, she might take a candidate to a plant nursery to look for plants for the Physicians Health office. The game is designed to reveal – using plants as a 'prop' – how the candidate collaborates on a vision. Unless the candidate interviews for a creative position, Sibson probably does not care if they favor a bougainvillea or a bonsai tree. In the improvisational interview, there are no right or wrong choices, only strong or weak ones. By creating a scene between that's real and happening in the moment, a candidate's qualities come to life as actions. Sibson's version of The Ride-Along game allows her to assess a candidate's ability to play with and nurture a vision, no matter what it is.

Naturally, Sibson's interview will cover professional credentials of the candidate. But she knows going in that those are good, or she wouldn't waste her time with the interview. As with most job openings, there are usually quite a few qualified candidates. Questions of baseline qualifications are often irrelevant. What Sibson wants revealed is who has the vision to play on the Physicians Health stage.

Note that 'vision' to an improvisational brand or a company like Physicians Health does not have the same meaning that it does for Industrial Age organizations. It does not mean leadership, foresight or repeatedly making the 'right' decisions regarding the direction of the company. It means, rather, the capacity for seeing and participating in the business, whether that business is plant selecting or health care, in a meaningful way.

Hot Seat. Essentially, the interviewer asks the candidate to 'walk the talk' by demonstrating proficiency in a skill described in his or her resume. Andy Henry, the head of the Disney Studios' Audio-Visual department, does this with the programmers and graphic designers who apply for jobs. "If somebody has on their resume that they are skilled in AfterEffects, and I'm thinking about hiring them, I'll walk them over to a workstation, sit them down, and give them half an hour to show me something," Henry says. As part of its interview process, the Red Bull energy drink company does 'group scenes' in which 20 candidates are put into rooms with no script and no instructions. Interviewers observe the group from behind a one-way mirror to see which people in the group have the best energy and are the most naturally gregarious. Candidates are then asked, one at a time, to give improvised speeches while the other candidates crawl toward the speaker and paw and shout at him or her like adoring fans. The Red Bull interviewers want to see who holds their composure the best, and who exhibits the most playfulness in the face of the unscripted, highly random situations their employees face at public promotions for the drink.

And then there's the classic version of Hot Seat game used by generations of interviewers for sales jobs. The interviewer picks up some random item from the room – an apple from a bowl of fruit, for example – and says, "Sell me this apple." The interviewer wants to see the quality of the communication that transpires during the pitch. Is the candidate 'connecting'? Is there emotion in the pitch? Does the candidate build a relationship with the interviewer or is the focus on the 'product'? These are answers to 'questions that cannot be asked', but *can* be ascertained through the *playing of the game*.

SALES

SOMETIMES, IN THE NEVERENDING IMPROVISATION that is business, your scene partner will also be your audience. A job interview is one example of this kind of scene. Lunch with the boss would be another. You engage your scene partner in pursuit of the objective, communicating as well as you can, adding useful information and finding the agreement that moves the scene forward. Then the scene partner, either immediately or shortly following, steps back into a different, critical role and assesses the scene's effectiveness at achieving the objective. A recruiter gives thumbs up or thumbs down. Your boss reviews your performance. But nowhere in business is this 'scene-partner-as- audience' dynamic more apparent or important than in *Sales* scenes.

Sales, as we all know, means everything to business. A sale is the ultimate 'applause' from your audience for the performance by you and your brand. In this chapter, I'm going to look at sales scenes from several perspectives: from that of the players involved in the scene; at the audience response that results in 'sale' or 'no sale'; and at different 'genres' of sales scenes. I'll also cite examples of outstanding salespeople and what makes them great.

Everyone sells. Whether you're an engineer emerging from your laboratory of wires and whatnots to seek funding for your latest brainstorm or you're a commission-only Key West condo time share realtor, you sell. The theater of business can be described as the drama of products and ideas in search of their audience and, having found the audience, its approval. That approval takes the form of a sale. There are as many selling styles as there are stars in the sky and as seemingly as many books about selling as there are sellers to buy them. But everything you've ever read, heard or experienced about selling can be distilled into the answer to a single question: How well do you improvise?

"All I *do* is improvise," says Tim Demarais, Senior Vice-President of Sales for ABRO Industries, a South Bend, Indiana-based exporter whose sales have grown from $5 million in 1980 to more than $100 million in 2007. "Our customers come from all over the world, speak different languages, live in different cultures. In our business, you never know what you're going to have to do to close a sale. I've ridden camels. I've eaten meals where I had no idea what I was being served. I've worn the local clothing. I've done deals with people when the two of us didn't speak a single word of each other's language." As Demarais points out, the art of selling, like the art of improvisation, comes down to communication – communication that often has very little to do with spoken language. The meaningful language lies elsewhere, encrypted in the behaviors and emotions of the customer. It is up to the seller to ferret this meaning from the customer's actions and, having identified it, act on it. Specifically, the meaning the seller seeks is what the customer wants.

What does the customer want? What matters to the audience in an improvisation scene is not what the players say, but what they mean and care about. What moves them? Causes them to act the way they do? These are the questions (and answers) that fascinate the audience, because they are what give the scene its life. If I play a cranky dad scolding my lazy son for the poor job he's doing mowing the yard, the audience does not care about the yard, how well or poorly it gets mowed, or whether it *ever* gets mowed. What they care about is *why* the people in the scene are acting the way they do. Why does it *matter* to the father how the yard gets mowed? When the audience learns that the father wants his son's respect and the one thing he knows is yard work, the scene takes on real meaning and the audience will come along for the ride. The question – the *dramatic problem* – posed by the scene, the thing that enables it to find its focus and move its players toward the objective, is whether or not the old man will get some respect. Fine, but what does this have to do with the art of selling? Here it is:

Your product is analogous to the yard mowing in the scene above. In and of itself, it holds no particular meaning for the audience beyond its utilitarian function.

When you sell (convince your audience to go along for the ride), it's not the yard mowing you sell. You are not selling a product. You are selling the *gratification of your scene partner's (customer's) desire.*

To make a sale, you give the customer what the customer wants. What the old man wants is respect. If you give him respect, the old man will pay you to mow the yard. That is how you close. Give the old man (your customer) what he wants and he will pay you for your product.

There is a successful plumbing company in Los Angeles, Mike Diamond Plumbing, that advertises on the radio that its plumbers smell good. It always makes me smile to hear it because it seems like sketch material for *Saturday Night Live* and, at the same time, ingenious advertising. As I do with every business scenario I come across, I think about it in terms of improvisation. Specifically, when it comes to this advertising, I ponder what Diamond Plumbing is *selling* to its customer audience. Is it a smell? If a you request a plumber from them, do you a choice of fragrances? No. That may be what Mike Diamond Plumbing is advertising, but it's not what they're selling. They are selling what the sweet-smelling plumber represents: respect for the customer, attention to detail and pride in appearance. The advertised product may be 'plumbers that smell good', but what the customer audience wants is *a good plumbing experience.* Mike Diamond's way of promising that is to represent it to the customer symbolically.

How Customers Become Buyers

As mentioned earlier in this chapter, sales scenes typically feature a player who 'becomes the audience' and passes judgment on the scene. Here's how it goes: You engage with the customer and build the relationship. All the rules for good scene work apply. *Listening* enables you to understand the customer's desire. *Movement* conveys excitement and meaning. *Emotion* connects you. And then, if all goes well, you ask for the order. At this instant, you are ending the scene and awaiting the audience's reaction. Did they love it? (Sale!) Do they applaud politely but not enthusiastically? (Maybe next time.) Or are they in a hurry to hit the exit? (No sale.) The aim of the improvisational salesperson is to engage the customer in such a delightful scene, one so well-played and firing on all cylinders, that when customer audience passes judgment, you'll have a sale.

Sales scenes can be as brief as a product demonstration or can span the entire lifetime of a personal relationship. *The longer the sales cycle, the more important the relationship between the scene partners.*

An impulse purchase taking a matter of seconds may involve only the most fleeting, ephemeral relationship between the customer and a brand.

A sales cycle that spans a lengthier period of time – let's say the decision to purchase a new car – will involve deeper relationships with both the automobile brand and the salesperson representing the brand. At a car dealership, a customer might forge a temporary relationship with the salesperson, but that's usually the extent of it. In all likelihood, you will not be having dinner with someone trying to sell you a car.

When the sales cycle spans many months, however, there are probably many dinners and other social settings involved. The scene will be much more complex, with many characters and many desires to be ferreted out and met. If it goes on long enough, a scene will become almost exclusively about the relationship. John Callahan, Sales Manager for GE's Automation division, which produces networked manufacturing systems, notes the importance of relationships in a long sales cycle: "What happens when there's that much money at stake – one of our systems might cost several million dollars – the customer knows your product almost as well as you do. There's very little you can tell them about what you're selling that they don't already know. So the question becomes 'What do you talk about?' Well, you talk about the relationship between your company and theirs, and between the people involved in making the system work."

Callahan further notes the importance of improvisation in building those relationships. "You cannot stick to a script. In a long sales cycle, if you try to stick to the script, you'll run out of things to say. You have to improvise by working with what your customers give you in the way of information about themselves." Callahan's description of how salespeople improvise could apply equally well to an improv theater performance. You 'work with what your scene partners give you in the way of information about themselves'.

When Tim Demarais and his ABRO Industries team were building their business in the late 1970s by opening new markets in Africa, the Middle East and Asia for their export goods, Demarais took it upon himself to crack the Nigerian market. He established a relationship with a customer in Nigeria named Prince Ben Moore Okoli. At first, as you might expect, the yearly sales were nothing to phone home about, barely enough to cover the cost of the travel, sometimes not even that. Then one day in 1979, Demarais received a phone call from Okoli in Lagos, who said that his niece, Margaret Anaba, enrolled at the time as a sophomore at Alabama A&M University, was twelve hundred dollars short on her tuition money for the spring semester and Okoli was having trouble wiring the money to the school. After the call, Demarais requested ABRO's management to front Ms. Anaba's tuition money. This move flew in the face of the commonly accepted business wisdom of the time that 'What goes into Nigeria does not come out'. Nevertheless, based on the relationship Demarais had built with Okoli, ABRO wired the money to Alabama A & M.

Not only did the tuition money get repaid, but Okoli soon activated new Nigerian distribution channels on ABRO's behalf and, by 1982, the company was selling $600,000 worth of product a year in Nigeria. The Nigerian audience was applauding. And the scene did not end there…

Late in 1982, Demarais got a vial of blood in the mail, postmarked Lagos, Nigeria. It was from Okoli. The blood was his father's. "To this day, I don't know how he got that through Customs," Demarais laughs. Okoli's father, from a remote Nigerian village, was in failing health and there were no doctors near enough to treat him, or even diagnose what might be wrong. "He wanted me to see if I could find a doctor here in the U.S. who'd run tests on the blood. Most wouldn't touch it. I finally found one who would. The tests showed three or four things wrong with the guy, the main one being diabetes."

On his next trip to Lagos, Demarais brought medicine, and he and Okoli drove nine hours from Lagos to reach Okoli's father's village. There, they found Okoli's father deathly ill and drinking palm wine as his remedy. "The man was a *diabetic*. The last thing he should have been doing was *drinking wine*," says Demarais. "We took the wine away from him, gave him the medicine, and before we left the village he was already starting to feel better." With his father's health restored, Okoli's participation in the ABRO scene heightened yet again. By 1983, ABRO was doing $2 million in sales a year in Nigeria. And the scene did not end there...

During the mid 1980s, Nigeria's economy crashed due to massive foreign exchange problems. During this period, ABRO's sales plummeted in Nigeria. Chief Ben Moore Okoli decided to get out of importing and into farming, as it was very difficult to get the exchange for imports. (ABRO's entire Nigerian revenue one year during this period was $750 – the cost of a player organ Okoli bought for his farmhouse.) The company had no distributor in Nigeria until one day in 1989 Demarais received a phone call from a familiar name – Margaret Anaba, who by now had a college degree, American citizenship and a job and home in Columbus, Ohio. She introduced Demarais and ABRO's owner and President, Peter Baranay, to her nephew, Dr. Cosmas Maduka. Maduka had become a prominent businessman when the Nigerian economy surged after the foreign exchange issue stabilized and was now the exclusive BMW and Ford Motor Company distributor for Nigeria. Maduka saw the sales potential of ABRO products and began promoting them throughout Nigeria on a weekly television infomercial (Demarais appeared on it several times) after which sales of ABRO products skyrocketed.

Today, ABRO Industries does over $20 million annually in Nigeria, their largest overseas market. The relationship with Demarais and the Maduka organization goes deeper than business. Seventy-two of Maduka's associates from Nigeria attended Demarai's father's funeral in South Bend, Indiana, in 2004.

Most U.S. companies are amazed at the volume that ABRO does in Nigeria today, as the country still presents one of the more challenging business climates in the world. What made ABRO's success possible is that Demarais and his colleagues understood early in their relationship that what Prince Ben Moore Okoli wanted was not just ABRO products but also an education for his niece and good health for his father. The language in which they communicated was a universal one – spoken not only in words, but in actions.

VII. PRACTICE

The taming of the mind, the dissolution of the ego, and
the letting go of all fears can only take place through patient practice.

— *Kenny Werner*

NINE EXERCISES

Superhero

THIS IS A GROUP EXERCISE that will appeal to anyone who grew up watching cartoons on TV – and who didn't? Having fun is the focus. By having fun, players drop preconceptions about learning and the usual subjective, self-judgmental baggage they bring to their scenes, and open themselves to the observations that can be made objectively about teamwork, the group mind, and giving and taking with energy.

Objective: Learning to give and take within a team.

Description: Players stand in a circle. By turns, each player says a made-up superhero name and accompanies the name with a signature gesture. (The superhero "Yo-Yo Boy," for example, might be accompanied by the player pantomiming yo-yoing wildly with both hands, "Hips Don't Lie" might be accompanied by a Shakira-style dance move). Once players have chosen their names, the group goes around the circle performing their superhero names in turn, and the entire group says the name and performs the signature gesture in unison. A couple of times around the circle and the players should remember everyone's superhero. Then they begin giving and taking. A player does his own superhero gesture followed by someone else's ("Yo-Yo Boy, Hips Don't Lie!"), passing to the other player, who repeats his or her own superhero name and signature gesture, then another, ("Hips Don't Lie, Vacuumulator!") and the group continues giving and taking around the circle.

Skills: Team building.

Coaching: Keep it moving. Don't get self-conscious. Don't laugh. You take yourself seriously as a superhero, you save the world on a regular basis. Use big gestures. Be heroic! Match each other's energy! Give with energy and take with energy!

Evaluation: This is primarily a warm-up exercise. But there's no improvisation that does not open doors to learning. At some point in the curriculum, the coach should ask the players to reflect on this particular exercise. What keeps the game lively? What makes it fun? What business situations can be improved by warming up first? What might our business presentations and other team-oriented situations be like if we give and take with this kind of energy?

Follow-Up: Once players become comfortable and adept with the game, the coach can suggest variations. Drop the names and give using only the signature gesture and a sound effect. Drop the sound effect and give with only the signature gesture. Now give with only the sound effect. Now morph the sound effect into something different but related to the original sound. The Superhero exercise can evolve into anything the players want it to be, as long as the principles of giving and taking with clarity, energy and focus are maintained.

Electric Company

This exercise is to improv what the *Sweet Georgia Brown* circle at center court is to the Harlem Globetrotters – an old standard, familiar and fun. Almost everyone who's had any improv training has done this exercise. As with most improv exercises, it is designed to let the mind to play freely, unfettered by the subjective questions we ask ourselves before taking action: Will this be silly? What will people think? Is this the best I can do? Will I look stupid? When you are learning, those kinds questions do not matter because they are irrelevant to the state of mind that makes learning possible.

Objective: Playing with words and group rhythm.

Description: Players form a circle and snap their fingers, swinging their arms back and forth in unison. With the rhythm established, one person says a word ("hot") and a person next to them adds to the word on the beat ("potato") to add meaning to the first word, thus creating a new concept. The group, on the beat, repeats the new word or phrase ("hot potato!") and then in unison sings the phrase from the old *Electric Company* children's TV show on PBS ("doot-doo-doo!"). The person who said "potato" says a new word, the person next to them adds to it, the group says the new two-word phrase and sings the phrase from *Electric Company* – all while keeping the beat with snapping fingers and swinging arms.

Skills: Openness to oneself, objectivity.

Coaching: Don't anticipate, because you can't. Don't think, just say the first thing that comes out of your mouth. If it's not a word in the dictionary, that's okay. Focus on the word you're given by the person next to you, not on the word with which you're going to respond. The taking is in the giving. The secret is in the game, not in your mind. Unlock the game. Play the game. The most important thing is to stay in rhythm. Gradually pick up the pace. Change the pace. How fast can you go?

Evaluation: How does the game change when the tempo slows down or speeds up? Note that the outcome of two words put together can perfectly well be a nonsense word or phrase ("rocket" plus "zombie" equals "rocket-zombie!"). This is fine. It's original. It gives players an insight as to how fresh business and branding ideas can be synthesized from seemingly disparate or unrelated concepts. "Stylish" plus "affordable" equals Target. "Fast food" plus "healthy" equals Subway. Doot-doo-doo!

Follow-Up: This exercise can be used as a warm-up for specific scenes, such as ad campaigns and product naming, that involve generating an original vocabulary.

Ten Things

Good improvisation works from what is 'seen' and not what is 'preconceived'. When we work from what we see, from what is true and real about a scene, we are more connected with our teammates. Our support means much more to the scene, and we are much more productive when we know what we are supporting. Like the best improv performers, the best business people work with what is real, not preconceived notions that block sight of what's really happening in a scene. This exercise helps players see what's real and allows them to share this reality with one another.

Objective: Working from what is observed in the moment, not what is decided beforehand.

Description: Players form a circle. One player names another player in the circle and directs them to "Name ten things…" that belong to a certain category ("ten things in the trunk of your car," "ten animals you'd see at the zoo"). The group counts out loud as each new thing gets named until the player has named ten things in the category. At this point, the entire group claps and counts to ten in unison. The player who named ten things assigns a different category to another player. Play continues until everyone in the circle has named ten things.

Skills: Seeing, working visually, working instinctively.

Coaching: Don't recite a list of things, see the place where those things exist and describe what you see. The list is in your head, what you see is real. We can all share it. Let your things describe the place. If the place is the trunk of your car, describe what you see there. If the ten things are brands of cereal, see the cereal aisle at the supermarket or a montage of TV commercials for cereals. See and describe! Don't think, see! Visualize! Where are the ten things? What's it like? What does it smell like? What does it sound like?

Evaluation: We can react much more instinctively and fluidly when we work with what we see instead of what we presume. Discuss the difference between seeing and preconceiving. How much harder is it to come up with ten words that fit into a category versus envisioning a space and describing what you see there? It is so much easier to think up one of something (the trunk of my car) than it is ten (things that other people will think well of me if I were to tell them that they are what I keep in the trunk of my car), so think of one and describe it! When we make a list, we are working from our intellect and ego, which edit the list ("belongs… doesn't belong…might belong if I can't think of something better in the next two seconds…") and passing subjective judgments on every single item. When, by comparison, we describe what we see, we are focusing on the objective (what is seen) meaning that others can see it, too. Sharing what is real is a much more productive path than preconceiving what is not.

Follow-Up: When the group gets familiar with the exercise, it can include business-themed categories ("ten things you do to hold down expenses," "ten things people leave in the lunchroom," "ten things everybody at work is talking about"). This exercise can also be used as a warm-up for scenes such as sales presentations that have specific objectives ("ten things this customer will like about our pitch," "ten great things about our product," "ten reasons we're ahead of the competition"). My improv team at the I.O. West Theater, Mud Hen, varies the exercise by changing the number of things to fewer than ten; or by clapping fast and quietly as the player names the ten things, allowing the clapping to crescendo with each new thing named, and picking up speed as we go.

Three-Line Scenes

The best improvisers have a keen sense of the 'Who, What and Where' of a scene. They understand the characters in the scene; they comprehend what the scene is about; and they are acutely aware of the environment in which the scene is transpiring. Unlike improv theater, where characters are created for specific scenes and the environment exists in the imagination, business scenes are obviously more rooted in reality. There is a real office with real furniture. There is real weather outside. People have real jobs and real lives. In business, the Who-What-Where is easier to comprehend and share. Still, think about the number of business scenes we've participated in where, beyond their boilerplate roles and responsibilities, we really did not know our scene partners very well. And think of the time spent trying to agree on what some business scenes are about, what they are meant to accomplish. This exercise helps players become more adept at establishing the factual foundation for their scenes. Agreement on the foundational facts of a scene gets it off to a much faster start and also allows it to evolve organically. If you have the Who-What-Where, you know you're on solid ground right at the top of your scene.

Objective: Establishing a factual foundation for a scene.

Description: Players form two lines on either side of the stage. The first two players take the stage. One initiates by establishing the Who ("Principal Stutz, you've got the wrong sophomore"), the second player makes a What statement ("Mr. Franks, we've never had someone killed in Kill Ball before, and the kids in the gym class say you did it"), after which the first player delivers a Where line ("And you think by bringing me back here to the gym,

I'm going to crack"). Three lines. Three facts. We know that a high school principle is investigating a Kill Ball murder allegedly committed by a sophomore student in a gym class, and that the student is claiming innocence. We further know that the scene is taking place in the gym. That's a lot of good information given in just three lines. The stage is set. The scene has the data it needs to evolve. Two new players take the stage and do another three-line scene depicting the Who-What-Where. The exercise continues until players begin to find conversational rhythms that let the information emerge naturally.

Skills: Introductions, setting the stage for productive scenes.

Coaching: Be specific. Who are you to one another? Listen. Let the What evolve naturally from the Who, and the Where from the Who and the What. The information you're giving is inevitable. You were involved in the What before the scene began. Don't start at the beginning of your story – begin in the middle. Don't invent – see. Players who initiate, make strong choices. Players who take the second line, don't anticipate. Work at listening, not scripting.

Evaluation: What kind of information is useful to share at the top of a meeting or business scene? What happens to scenes when the Who-What-Where is not established early? What do we typically not know about Who our scene partners are that would help get scenes off to a better start? How is the Where important to business scenes? Cite examples of meetings or scenes in which the What did not get clarified, and the effect that had. If you could know anything about a customer to help you close a sale, what would that information be?

Follow-Up: As players get more comfortable with the rhythms of the exercise, they should begin to use business-related facts for the foundation. As the exercise evolves towards real world scenarios, the restriction of three lines should be lifted, without losing the focus of imparting three pieces of factual information. Add more players to the exercise, so that there's more to the Who. Substitute 'When' for Where. Recognize that the factual information necessary for a business scene may involve more than the basic requirements for the exercise. Point out that the exercise is designed to create awareness of the need to build business scenes on solid, agreed-upon information.

Twenty Characters in Two Minutes

The idea of playing a character in business contrasts with what improv performers do onstage in the sense that in business the objective is to embrace who you are as a person, your strengths and attributes as a human being; in improv theater, you use who you are as the raw material for characters who can entertain the audience because of what they represent. In improv theater, character is metaphorical. In the improvisation of business, character is real. This exercise is designed to stretch our understanding of who we are, to develop our 'vocabulary of authentic behaviors' so that we can be the most effective version of ourselves for any given scene. Most of us have the ability to be a lot more entertaining, animated, engaging and interesting than we let on. We can use more inflection and modulation in our voices than we normally do. We can use our hands more to describe things. We can be more aware of how we stand and move. This exercise will help players see themselves as they are and as they have the potential to be.

Objective: Building character, animation, self-expression.

Description: Players form a circle. One player takes the center. The rest of the group shouts out characters for the player in the center to play. The player quickly assumes the characters suggested by the group. The coach times the group and counts the number of characters performed by the player in the center. The goal of the exercise is to average a new character every six seconds, thus completing 20 characters in two minutes.

Skills: Communication, self-awareness.

Coaching: Focus on doing one thing that each character would do. Don't think, do! Become! Use your body and your posture. How would these characters stand? Let your posture and pose dictate what comes out of your mouth. Go big right away – you don't have time to start small. Strike a new pose for each character. Jump into each new character. Players in the circle, give strongly. Player in the center, take strongly. The objective is not to entertain, the objective is to do 20 characters in two minutes. Stay focused on the objective.

Evaluation: Talk about the importance of character in business. (See the *Character* chapter for review.) What characters stuck in people's minds and why? When did giving strongly by someone in the circle lead to taking strongly by the person in the center? When was the suggested character so strong that the player in the center 'got it' immediately? How does the exercise reveal a person's communication skills and personality? What poses or moves led us to see a character before a word was spoken? Use the exercise to stretch your potential for expressing yourself.

Follow-Up: After players are comfortable and adept with the exercise, perform it with characters who populate the business environment ("Cranky Customer!" "Auditor" "Computer Geek," "Chairman of the Board," "Head of Sales!" etc.). Perform the exercise with the members of the group naming business situations for the player in the center to enact *as themselves* ("Stuck in an Elevator," "Trying to Get the Copy Machine to Work," "Drinks with the Boss," etc.). And of course, for some laughs and lighthearted play, there's always the silly, chaotic version of this exercise: 'Twenty Characters in a Minute'.

Build a Brand

What is more important to the long-term livelihood of an organization than establishing a brand identity? This exercise takes the years-long process of honing a company's value-driven behaviors and condenses it into a game that lasts a matter of minutes. It encourages players to think about branding as a lively interplay of ideas from many different points-of-view, as a non-hierarchical mosaic and as a network that shapes itself around a product or service.

Objective: Branding a product or idea.

Description: The coach names a product. Members of the group stand in a semicircle and envision the product before their eyes, describing its attributes, suggesting names for it and ideas for how to sell it – anything, in short, that makes the product appealing to its 'intended market'. The exercise continues until the objective has been realized. Initially, the products should be fanciful ("a personal blimp," "mini-kangaroos," etc.) so that players won't be hindered by their subjective views toward existing genres of products ("a children's theater," "a laundry detergent," etc.).

Skills: Teamwork, collaboration, ideation.

Coaching: See the product and work with it. What does it look like? What makes it great? What is unusual about it? Why will people love it? What is its appeal? Who is the competition and why will your product kick the competition's ass? Give me the TV commercial for it. Give me the billboard ad. If you're the kind of person who's into this sort of product, what are you going to say about it? What celebrities will endorse it? What would they say about it? What is the experience of this product? The product connects the group. You have it in common. You're excited about it.

Evaluation: How is the exercise analogous to the building of a real brand? What things did you see in the exercise that you see in real business scenarios? What was the brand that you built? Did the product get a name? Did you agree on what it looked like? Did you agree on the market for the product? What ideas were unexpected, memorable or compelling? Why? Was there a big-time marketing hook? How was the product to be sold? Was your pitch technical or emotional? Was this going to be a media-driven brand or would it rely on word-of-mouth?

Follow-Up: As players get more comfortable, the exercise evolves naturally into real world product genres, and then into the organization's own products or services. The coach must be careful, as the real world scenarios are introduced, to preserve the free play that characterizes the game when fanciful products are given. The breakthroughs around a brand occur when the intensity of our focus propels us through the walls of preconception into the territory where creativity can spontaneously combust. It is easy to have no preconceptions about a mini-kangaroo; it is much more difficult to operate with no preconceptions about your own product. It takes practice and discipline.

Gibberish Scenes

'Gibberish' is nonsense language. (The statement, "Landi lo brunga ridda-ski pela-ski" is gibberish.) There are countless variations of gibberish exercises for the improviser, all rooted in Viola Spolin's early work in childhood development. They all have the benefit of helping players develop and communicate with their non-language skills. In the Networked World, with business communication so heavily textual, non-language skills become more important than ever. Communicators who can speak with emotion and listen to more than just words are going to be in high demand. Gibberish exercises provide powerful training for all business people, especially for those in sales, marketing and communication.

Objective: Communicating effectively without relying on language.

Description: One player assumes the role of Salesperson, while another plays the Buyer/Audience. The Salesperson makes a sales presentation in gibberish, the Buyer responds in gibberish, the scene continues until the objective has been reached.

Skills: Sales, one-to-one communication, physicality.

Coaching: Be animated. Be overly animated. Speak with your body. Use your hands. Demonstrate. Let your body take on the attributes of the product. Move your feet like a dancer. Use the stage. Let what you're saying flow through your mind, but don't let your mind get in your way. Be specific. Make distinct sounds in a made-up language. Make eye contact. Don't stare. Forget what's coming out of your mouth and focus on everything else. Communicate from your gut. Make it as meaningful as you can. Use everything you've got! Don't sell, pitch! Pitch as if your life depends on selling this product!

Evaluation: What did you feel when you were doing each? What did it look like from the audience's point of view? What did you notice about your body? What is the difference between selling and pitching? What did the scene look like when the players were communicating effectively? How did that compare with when they were not?

Follow-Up: More players join the Buyer's side onstage, so that there are multiple Buyers and a single Salesperson. Repeat with multiple Salespeople/multiple Buyers and multiple Salespeople/single Buyer. All Buyers step offstage and the Salesperson/ Salespeople present to everyone in the room. Repeat the exercise, using real words this time, and matching them to the organic movement and energy level from the gibberish presentation. The exercise can be done with many different kinds of business-related scenes – job interviews, HR (e.g. sexual harassment scenarios) and brainstorming, to name a few. Any business scenario can be better understood and any presentation can be made more compelling by rehearsing with gibberish.

Geico Pitch

This game was used in 2006-07 to good effect in U.S. television spots for Geico Auto Insurance. In these 30-second spots, a typical Geico customer would relate a banal story of an automobile in need of repair, a dry recitation of the facts, which would get interpreted into an entertaining story by recognizable celebrity performers like Little Richard, Vern Troyer and Charo. Geico's spots are simply a variation of a tried-and-true improv exercise.

Objective: Bringing information to life, seeing the difference between cold data and compelling communication.

Description: Two players take the stage. One tells a story using only the facts, recited without emotion or embellishment ("My grandpa took me fishing…"). The second player dramatizes the story as a performance using emotion, character and other elements of the improvisation techniques ("One balmy day in May, before the sun was up, my grandfather shook me awake and said, 'Get your lazy ass out of bed, the trout are running!'"). The exercise should continue for approximately two minutes or until the story peaks.

Skills: Sales, presentations, branding, communicating with emotion.

Coaching: Paint a picture. Use emotion! Engage us. Why do we care? What is happening in the scene? What does it feel like? What does it smell like? Where is it happening? What is your attitude toward the events in the story?

Evaluation: Ask the group to describe the differences between the facts and the performance. Are both equally true? What is the effect on the audience? How did each of the two versions of the story make us feel? What is being communicated in one version that is absent from the other? Why is pitching important? What is the difference between selling and pitching? Are there situations in business when a simple recitation of the facts is preferable to a pitch? If so, when? What are some business scenarios in which a pitch is the preferred way of communicating?

Follow-Up: Players should begin doing this exercise with stories not related to work, and gradually integrate work scenarios such as sales pitches and presentations into the mix. Successful business people, from scientists with a compelling vision of the cosmos to lawyers who win cases, are good at pitching. Most people don't have any trouble figuring out *what* to pitch; the challenge is figuring out *how*. This exercise will help you discover how to pitch effectively.

Hidden Desire

If the players and audience alike are engaged by the onstage efforts to understand and fulfill desires, then the scene will be a good one, guaranteed. Active, effective scenes are often about the seductive interplay in the margins of the scene, expressed with unspoken eloquence. 'Hidden Desire' is designed to expand the players' listening skills and also brings to light, for the players and the class who are observing, how our behaviors are the code for our unstated desires.

Objective: Understanding motivation.

Description: The coach hands slips of paper to two players, each with a hidden desire written on it ("I want a hug," "I want a hamburger" etc.). The players are given a suggestion, such as a place, and begin a conversation. The hidden desire cannot directly stated – it must reveal itself organically through the behaviors and conversation of the players. Players continue until the objective is apparent or the coach determines that it's out of reach. As always with the *GameChangers* exercises, I recommend beginning with playful scenarios unrelated to business and gradually, as players get more comfortable and adept at the exercise, working business scenarios into the mix.

Skills: Sales, negotiations, job interviews, CRM.

Coaching: What was just done? Use your eyes. Use your bodies. Forget the words you're speaking, let the meaning come from what you feel. Move! You have to touch the other person to talk to them. How do you touch one another? Show, don't tell.

Evaluation: What were the hidden desires? How were they being communicated? What did you do? What did you see? If the hidden desires were not communicated, why not? If they were, how? Did you feel your behaviors connect with your desires? When? Were the players able to sustain the normal flow of conversation while also communicating their hidden desires?

Follow-Up: As stated earlier, the hidden desires will evolve into business situations ("I want compliments for my work," "I want to cut costs," etc.) with the players, class and coach evaluating scenes not only for their effectiveness in terms of improvisation, but also discussing what they bring to light about business communication. As players become more experienced, they can name their own hidden desires, written on slips of paper they hand to the coach. A variation of this game is known as 'One Unusual Thing'. It follows the same general structure, except that the hidden thing is an unusual fact about a player ("I am ambidextrous," "I just won the lottery" etc.).

GLOSSARY

Addition
The action of entering a scene in progress for the purpose of immediately contributing information or ideas to support the group's performance

Agreement Principle
The bedrock principal of improvisational business, characterized by players' openness towards each other within a scene and throughout a business organization's performance

Audience
Those within and outside of a business organization whose reactions and opinions will determine the success of a scene or performance

Being a Character
Displaying personality traits that make a player unique as an individual and that are beneficial to conducting business

Blocking
A performance-related problem that occurs when players impede the progress of a scene by refusing the gifts offered them by their teammates

Callback
The act of recalling information that was stated by a player earlier in a scene or in a previous scene

Cast
The assembly of players within a scene who share the same business-related objective; also called a group or team

Casting
The process of selecting players who will comprise a business team.

Character
The personality traits, skills and values that make a player unique and valuable to the team.

Coach
A person who casts a team; one who observes, and directs players toward achieving a business related-objective during preparation and/or performance of a scene

Cosmetic Communication
The surface level of transmitting and receiving information within a scene, primarily through dialogue

Denying
A form of blocking in which a player repeatedly contradicts or ignores other players, confusing the audience and fellow players

Edit
The action of making an entrance for the purpose of shifting the scene's focus, or to begin a new scene; edits usually occur in tandem with other players exiting the scene

Emotional Communication
A profound level of transmitting and receiving information within a scene, hinging on the recognition and fulfillment of a scene partner or audience's deep-rooted wants and needs

Energy
The pitch at which a player or group carries out (and modulates) its performance; an umbrella term for the level of activity and intensity the audience observes in the group, and that players in the group feel from one another

Entrance
The manner by which a player or group appears within a scene; there may be multiple entrances by the same player during a scene; also synonymous with the *initial* entrance by a player in a scene

Environment
Any setting in which members of an organization can collaborate to achieve a business related-objective; any place where players interact; more expansively, any place where an audience experiences a brand

Exit
The manner by which a player or group leaves a scene, either momentarily or for the duration of a scene; there may be multiple exits by the same player during a scene; also synonymous with the *final* exit of a player or group

External Audience
Those outside of a business organization whose judgment will determine the effectiveness of a scene; can consist of customers, competitors, government, media, etc.

Flatlining
A performance-related problem that occurs when players show no energy or life, impeding or halting a scene's progress

Game
Any tactic employed by a player or group ostensibly for the purpose of achieving a business-related objective; games fall into two broad categories – productive and unproductive

GameChanger
A player who has mastered the practical techniques of improvisational business

Gift
A move that supports the scene and the players in it

Global Environment
The overall business climate in which an organization operates, shaped by factors such as regulatory agencies, competitors, disruptive geopolitical factors and the desires, attitudes and beliefs of customers

Crazy Town
A performance-related problem that occurs when the fantasizing in a scene gets out of hand, until

it becomes un-moored from any comprehensible frame of reference

Grandstanding
A performance-related problem that occurs when a player wastes time and effort trying to contribute something 'heroic' to a scene; holding back for effect instead of engaging in the moment

Group Mind
The tangible web of connectivity between players; achieved through a shared focus on the scene's objective

Having Character
Possessing positive and desirable virtues and values, such as honesty, integrity, commitment and trust, that are essential to conducting business

Heighten
To build emotional involvement and energy within a scene

Improvisation
Interpersonal and group communication that is both instinctive and informed by experience, knowledge and awareness of the world

In-Between Character
A player or a players' traits and values that halt a scene's progress through unreliability and the habitual unwillingness to make a decision or express a clear, unambiguous idea

Initiation
The first meaningful words or lines spoken during a scene; in this case, 'meaningful' refers to anything that directly involves the group's progress toward achieving the scene's objective

Internal Audience
Those within a business organization or an industry whose judgment determines the effectiveness of a scene

Interrogation
A performance-related problem that occurs when a player only asks questions and never does anything with the information revealed by the answers

Fantasizing
A performance-related problem that occurs when a player does not acknowledge or deal with the facts of a scene

Invocation
A style of group opening that identifies the themes for a performance; while improv comedy uses a very specific, four-beat format, the variation in business can be any process that lets players move from a third-person to first-person connection with the ideas that generate themes

Issue
Any performance-related problem which can be remedied by better execution of fundamental *GameChangers* improvisational business techniques

Judging
A performance-related problem that occurs when a player assesses the merits of a scene while that scene is taking place

Justifying
A performance-related problem that occurs when a player makes excuses or self-consciously explains the state of a scene or situation related to the scene

Meta-Communication
A scene's representation of issues, ideas, or concerns that exist on a societal or universal level, such as a global trend, widely held belief or aspect of the human condition

Monologue
A speech given by a single player in a scene; paradoxically, a monologue can be shared amongst multiple players in the course of an opening or presentation

Negative Character
A player or a player's traits and values that halt a scene's progress through skepticism and a disagreeable inclination to oppose, deny and/or resist the ideas or involvement of other players

Networked World
The highly communicative, internet-supported global stage on which business gets conducted

Objective
The desired outcome of a scene; the focus of a scene; the business goal of a scene

Opening
An 'overture' prior to a scene or series of scenes in which a player or a group develops the themes for an upcoming performance; begins with a suggestion from the audience

Organic Opening
A style of group opening in which a 'stream-of-consciousness' dialogue and/or actions identify the themes for an coming performance

Organizational Environment
The overall physical presentation of a business to its audience

Pandering
A performance-related problem that occurs when a player appeals to an audience's baser instincts; in improv comedy, this is known as 'going for the easy laugh'

Performance
The sum total of actions taken by a player or group in a scene or series of scenes towards achieving a business-related objective

Pimping
A performance-related problem that occurs when a player makes an unreasonable demand or sets unreasonable expectations of other players

Play
Participation in a game or scene to achieve a shared objective

Player
Anyone who collaborates with others to achieve an objective

Role
The set of job-related responsibilities and duties for a specific player within a scene; playing a role is often colloquially referred to as 'wearing a hat'

Scene
Any interaction between two or more players who share an objective

Scene Partner
Anyone with whom a player interacts during a scene

Scenic Environment
The settings for the day-to-day conduct of business by an organization's employees

Scripting
A performance-related problem that occurs when a player plans how a scene will go beforehand, then sticks to the 'script', even if unforeseen events within the scene call for

actions different than those planned

Suggestion From the Audience
Any idea or piece of information given to the group prior to a performance by those who will judge the effectiveness of that performance; includes market research, customer relationship management, strategic imperatives, directions from a superior, etc.

Symbolic Movement
An action taken by a company or employee of a company that resonates beyond the scene or scenes in which it occurs (See *Meta-Communication*)

Theme
An idea generated in an opening that provides the inspiration and foundation for a scene or performance. Often related to a company's brand

Upstaging
The action of stealing focus from or negating the contributions of another player for self-aggrandizement

Yes-Anding
Agreeing with a scene partner's reality or declaration, then adding useful information or contribution of your own in order to arrive at a new idea or reality shared by the group

INDEX

NOTES

YOU ARE AN IMPROVISER

p. 20 Mick Napier's book gives an excellent feel of what's it like to improvise, in good scenes and bad ones, too. Mick Napier, *Improvise: Scene from the Inside Out*, 2004.

p. 20 Roger Fishman quotes are from a personal interview at Zizo offices, 2007.

p. 22 Jane Kleinberger quotes are from a telephone interview, 2007.

THE NETWORKED WORLD

p. 23 Jim Stengel P & G reference is from "The World on a String," by John Galvin, *Advertising Age/ 'Point'* supplement, 2005. The supposition that something unscripted, hence improvised, took the place of agency storyboard presentations is mine.

p. 24 Richard Taylor quote is from conversations we had during the production of *TRON*, 1982.

GAMES

p 41 Everything that has happened in improvisation in the past 75 years has its roots in a foundation of teaching by Viola Spolin and her mentor, Neva Boyd. Source here is "Viola Spolin," *Wikipedia*, http://wikipedia.org/wiki/Viola_Spolin, 2007.

p. 44 David LaPlante quote is from a personal interview at Twelve Horses offices, 2007.

p. 46 Samuel Shem, *House of God*, 1979

p. 47 Harrison Ellenshaw personal interview, Santa Barbara, California, 2001.

p. 49 Information about Ted Turner comes from CNN Online/ archived *Money* magazine article from 2003. http://money.cnn.com/2003/05/05/news/turner_aol/, 2007.

p. 49 Lizzie Widhelm telephone interview interview, July 2007.

p. 50 Noe Sanchez personal interview, 2007.

PLAYERS
p. 59 The story about Walt Disney comes from research that included personal interviews with dozens of contemporaries of Walt Disney, for *Walt*, a four-part mini-series I co-wrote with L. G. Weaver for the Walt Disney Company. 1984.

p. 60 The value of 20 shares of c. 1950 Disney stock courtesy Dave Smith, Chief Archivist, The Walt Disney Company.

AGREEMENT
p. 74 Viola Spolin, *Improvisation for the Theater*, 1960.

p. 74 Fishman, personal interview, 2007.

LISTENING
p. 77 Margaret J. Wheatley, *Listening as Healing*, http://www.margaretwheatley.com/articles/listeninghealing.html, 2007

p. 77 Wayne Allwine quotes are from personal conversations and interviews during the production of the *Disney Family Album* series, 1982.

MOVEMENT
p. 87 I re-experienced Steve Ballmer's legendary dance via *YouTube*, http://www.youtube.com/watch?v=XMrhoOHNOrI, 2007.

p. 88 Drs. Antonio and Hannah Damasio lecture, USC's Annenberg School of Communications, Los Angeles, 2006.

GROUP MIND

p. 105 The Kevin Wall quotes and *Live Earth* observations are excerpted from many conversations I had with him during the production of *Live Earth – Concerts for a Climate in Crisis*, for which I was Chief Storyteller, 2006-7.

p. 107 Ernest Hemingway, *To Have and Have Not*, 1970.

CHARACTER

p. 111 Song lyrics are from *Ac-Cent-Tchu-Ate the Positive*, Harold Arlen and Johnny Mercer, Capitol-EMI, 1944.

p. 112 My long association with the Walt Disney Company introduced me to lots of luminaries, including Ray Bradbury. This quote comes from a conversation I had with him in 1982.

p. 116 Nate Chapnick, "Ingvar Kamprad," *ForbesAutos*, 2005, http://www.forbesautos.com/advice/toptens/billionaire/05-ingvar_kamprad.html, 2007

SUGGESTIONS FROM THE AUDIENCE

p. 132 Information about the early days of Chicago improv are from Jeffrey Sweet's outstanding oral history of the art form, *Something Wonderful Right Away*, 2003.

p. 135 Taryn Rose research comes from my own Taryn Rose shoes, and from "25 Women Busness Builders," *Fast Company*, 2005.

p. 135 Tamara Sibson information and quotes are from a personal interview, Physicians Health offices, 2007.

p. 136 Jim Stengel quotes are from "Teaching an Old Dog New Tricks" by Patricia Sellers, *Fortune*, 2004, http://money.cnn.com/magazines/fortune/fortune_archive/2004/05/31/370714/index.htm, 2007

INITIATIONS
p. 142 Charna Halpern, *Art by Committee* DVD starring (among many other great improvisers) Tina Fey and Amy Poehler, 2006.

p. 148 The Disney story comes from recordings vaulted in The Walt Disney Company Archives recorded by journalist Pete Martin in 1954 for the book *My Dad, Walt Disney*, by Diane Disney Miller. Diane has herself told me several stories about her father over the years, which have added to my characterizations of him here and elsewhere in the book.

ENTRANCES, EXITS
p. 157 Bob King personal interview, The Walt Disney Company, 1983.

ISSUES
p. 163 When he wasn't flipping me the bird about a million times (our little inside joke), Aaron Grosky gave me generous insights into what it took to book the massive Live Earth event. Personal interviews, *Live Earth* offices, Los Angeles, 2006-7.

p. 169 "Elaine May," *Wikipedia*, http://en.wikipedia.org/wiki/Elaine_May, 2007

p. 169 "Follow the fear" is a very well known improv saying atrtributed to Del Close, documented by his friend and business partner, Charna Halpern, in her book, *Art By Committee*, 2006.

p. 169 Garrison Keillor personal interview, St. Paul, Minnesota, 1984.

COACHING
p. 177 Viola Spolin, *Improvisation for the Theater*, 1960.

SALES
p. 192 Tim Demarais quotes and story are from a series of telephone interviews, 2007.

p. 193 Mike Diamond Plumbing web site, http://www.mikediamondplumbing.com, 2007

NINE EXERCISES
The exercises in this chapter are adapted for business education from classic exercises performed by improv groups all around the world. Games-as-communication are as old as human history, but the modern theories, including those expressed in this book, have their origins in Neva Boyd and Viola Spolin's life's work, documented in Spolin's classic *Improvisation for the Theater*.

ACKNOWLEDGEMENTS

NO WORK OF IMPROVISATION, be it a performance or a book, would be possible without the groundwork laid by Viola Spolin, the godmother of modern improv, and her mentor, Neva Boyd. Spolin's classic book, *Improvisation for the Theater*, set the stage for generations to come. In being deeply indebted to her, I am far from alone and in very good company…

Authors Stephen Nachmanovitch (*Free Play*), Mick Napier (*Improvise*) Charna Halpern (*Truth in Comedy*; *Art by Committee*), Keith Johnstone (*Impro*) Janet Coleman (*The Compass*) Kenny Werner (*Effortless Mastery*) and Jeffrey Sweet (*Something Wonderful Right Away*) further guided my inquiry into the form and its history.

Charna Halpern, keeper of the improv flame, deserves extra thanks for creating the I. O. Theaters in Chicago, Charlotte and Los Angeles. The talented players at the I. O. West Theater in Los Angeles have changed my world. Thanks to James Grace, who manages I. O. West, and to my brilliant teachers there – Sara Gee, Erik Hunnicutt, Jason Pardo, Aaron Krebs, Michael Bertrando, Craig Cackowski, Shulie Cowen, Scot Robinson, Karen Graci, Ali Davis, Dave Hill and Shelley Berman. Thanks to Paul Vaillancourt for telling me where to look. A standing ovation for my teammates past and present in Mud Hen! – Adam Jeffries! Jill Czarnowski! Jennie Pierson! Harrison Brown! Melissa Sorrentino! Trevor Luce! Joy Allen! Eve Savona! Brian O'Connell! Bryan Truong! Sunah Bilsted! Chad Reinhart! Todd Basil! Ben Leddick!

Jeff Hawkins! Bouquets to our coaches, John Abbott and Nick Armstrong. And a rose to Mary Forrest for telling me about I. O. in the first place.

In 2003, Brian Murphy took the big leap into improv classes at Dad's Garage Theater in Atlanta, and our subsequent discussions convinced me there was material for this book. Dill and Susan Driscoll, owners of Ignition, Inc., in Atlanta, provided the first laboratory for GameChangers research in early 2004. Kevin Wall demonstrated the principles daily during the production of *Live Earth*, and let me get close enough to get burned when I wasn't careful. I treasure our friendship and the many amazing business scenes we've shared.

Thanks to Harrison Ellenshaw, Richard Taylor, John Lasseter and the teams behind *TRON* and *Toy Story* for giving me my first glimpses into the Networked World. Thanks to Diane Disney Miller for sharing stories and insights about her father, and to Dave Smith of the Disney Archives for letting me listen to the good stuff.

Thanks to the GameChangers who helped (and continue to help) shape the curriculum, especially Tamara Sibson, Tim Demarais, Jerry Steinhilber, Geoff Ratte, John Beiter, Cindy-Ann Hersom, Roger Fishman, Lizzie Widhelm, John Callahan, Rudy Ruettiger, David LaPlante, Martin Gastanaga, Steve Spencer, Jennifer Gardner and Noe Sanchez.

Thanks to Leilani Schweitzer for the GameChangers logo and the cover of this book, and to Monika Stout for the layout. Thank you, Carly Kuhn and Holly Hannula, for keeping the office in order while pursuing your own dreams. Jon Karas of Infinity Management has been in my corner through thick and thin. Thanks to Art Swerdloff, for everything, forever.

Dr. Virginia Kuhn of USC's Institute for Multimedia Literacy consulted closely with me on the pedagogical aspects of the program. Charles Lynn Frost, educator, actor, gentleman, devoted his extremely valuable time to reading and discussing early drafts. Patrick Jong Taylor knocked it out of the park with his editing of the text. His talent and perspective never failed to light the way.

And as always, endless thanks and deepest love to my family.

M. B.
09.07.07

ABOUT THE AUTHOR

MIKE BONIFER GREW UP ON A FAMILY FARM near Ireland, Indiana, and graduated from the University of Notre Dame. In his working life, he has played the roles of farmer, construction worker, sales representative, journalist, author, publicist, cable television producer, small business owner, documentary filmmaker, infomercial director, advertising copywriter, reality television segment producer, screenwriter, feature film director, web site producer and internet entrepreneur. The organizational hats he has worn include Creative Director, Vice President of Creative, Senior Vice President of Creative, Senior Vice President of Creative Worldwide, President and Chief Storyteller. He is the founder and CEO of GameChangers, LLC, an education company that uses improvisation techniques to help clients achieve their business goals.

WWW.GAMECHANGERS.COM

EARLY PRAISE FOR GAMECHANGERS

As the narratives of life and business become interconnected in a socially conscious world, the need for intuitive adaptability is imperative. This work truly dimensionalises how today's value driving performance is attached to a new set of dexterous and practised go-to-market behaviours.

Cindy-Ann Hersom
Brand Director, Community + Environment, The Coca Cola Company

In my law practice, I'm constantly encountering unexpected situations and being called upon to respond effectively and quickly. All of the legal research is for naught if you can't improvise with it, and in my twenty years before the bar, I've found that the truly great lawyers are all great improvisers. *GameChangers* gives the reader a powerful lens for seeing what makes people successful in all walks of life.

John C. Beiter
Partner, Loeb & Loeb

Bonifer just wrote the definitive counter-culture business book. While every other business sage focuses on planning, scripting and rehearsing, Bonifer's *GameChangers* articulates the very secret of every entrepreneur's success: improvisation is simply the best way to navigate today's dynamic and socially networked business world.

David LaPlante, CEO, Twelve Horses, Inc.

As an educator focused on the affordances of the networked world, I try to teach my students *how* to learn rather than *what* to learn. *GameChangers* is a brilliantly conceived, educationally sound, thoroughly relevant system for learning. Twenty-first century life requires the sort of flexibility and resourcefulness the *GameChangers* techniques provide. Anyone working in today's climate stands to benefit profoundly from its concepts and practices.

Virginia Kuhn, PhD
Institute for Multimedia Literacy, University of Southern California

Mike Bonifer takes the reader on an E-ticket ride into the future of business communications. Combining valuable life lessons and experiences from the worlds of entertainment, the internet, and improvisational comedy, he demonstrates how to step far outside the box of conventional thinking to sell campaigns, products, and ideas.

Howard E. Green
Vice President, Studio Communications, The Walt Disney Studios

It helps us build the product we wish to have, and create the experience we desire. Not pitted apart, not working disjointly, not dis-incentivized, but about all of us being a team. With the *GameChangers* techniques, we're smart and we're complete. Together.

Tamara Sibson
Co-Founder and President, Physicians Health Association/MMI